Author

Kerry Lewis has been a member of the mrbruff.com team since May 2014 when she published the first edition of this guide, which became an immediate hit on Amazon. She has also written Mr Bruff's guides to A' Level English Literature, *Jane Eyre* and *Animal Farm*. Kerry has co-written guides with Mr Bruff to *The Tempest* and *Julius Caesar*. You can follow her on Twitter @Mrs_SPaG.

Dedication

Mr Bruff would like to thank those who have helped and supported along the way:

- Sam Perkins, who designed the front cover of this eBook
- Sunny Ratilal, who designed the original front cover which was adapted for this edition

Kerry Lewis would like to thank Andrew Simmons for his help with proofreading the first edition of this guide. She would also like to thank Molly and Erin for their patience.

Copyright

First published 2014 by Andrew Bruff
This edition published 2018 by Andrew Bruff

Contents

First published in 2014, the original version of this guide aimed to review the basics of spelling, punctuation and grammar. Targeting native speakers of English, it was a revision tool to support GCSE English language.

Not long after publication, it became a statutory requirement for primary schools to teach to a new national curriculum that included more advanced grammar than anything that had previously been studied by most GCSE students. The basics were no longer good enough. The government even revamped the SPaG acronym (spelling, punctuation and grammar), rebranding it as EGPS (English grammar, punctuation and spelling).

In 2015, more marks became available for accurate spelling, punctuation and grammar in the new GCSE specification in English language. For the first time, marks for technical accuracy were also allocated to the GCSE in English literature.

This updated edition has been written in response to changes in the national curriculum, so it assumes some knowledge of previous study at Key Stage 2. The chapters are progressive, allowing students to work in a logical sequence, revising and building on their skills.

The guide can be used in three ways:

1. Between Years 7-9, to revise and build on Key Stage 2 English grammar, punctuation and spelling.
2. Between Years 10-11, to support a programme of revision and consolidation of previous learning.
3. Alternatively, it's a useful self-study revision aid for students who are preparing for their GCSE exam in English language.

Many people think that grammar is boring. It's not. This guide contains examples from literature to illustrate points; if students can see grammar in action, they are more likely to imitate techniques in their own writing. For those who like to be stretched and challenged, there's also a bonus chapter of advanced rhetorical techniques.

To develop an awareness of how spelling, punctuation and grammar evolved (plus other interesting bits and pieces), there are some *Fascinating Facts!* Oh, and apologies in advance for my sense of humour.

Kerry Lewis
@Mrs_SPaG

Chapter 1: Sentence Functions and Punctuation Basics

Question:	**Why does punctuation always end up in court?**
Answer:	**To be sentenced.**

In this chapter, we'll review the four purposes of sentences. Then we'll revise the punctuation marks that make these purposes clearer.

SENTENCE FUNCTIONS

All sentences have one of four purposes, called *functions*:

Declarative: a statement
Example: I read every day.

Interrogative: a question
Example: Do you read every day?

Imperative: a command
Example: Read every day!

Exclamatory: an exclamation
Example: I read every day!

Test Yourself!

Read the sentences, which describe the fascinating history of English grammar teaching. Label each sentence as declarative, interrogative, imperative or exclamatory.

1. Did you know that the word *grammar* comes from the Greek word *gramma*, which means *written character*?

2. The Greeks believed that grammar was good for developing logical thinking and speaking skills.

3. In the eighteenth century, people analysed English grammar by using Latin grammar rules!

4. Look it up if you don't believe me!

5. In the early 20th century, the standard of grammar teaching in schools became so bad that some people wanted to drop it from the curriculum.

6. It wasn't the fault of teachers—hardly anyone knew what English grammar was because there wasn't any university research on it.

7. Did you know that there was also a campaign to promote literature as an alternative to grammar?

8. From the 1960s, most schools stopped teaching English grammar!

9. Despite universities opening language and linguistics departments, students from other countries ended up knowing more about English grammar rules than native English speakers!

10. From the 1990s onwards, governments have recommended that English grammar be taught in schools.

Now check your answers on the next page.

Joke Break
A question mark walks up to an exclamation mark and asks, "Surprised to see me?"

1. Interrogative
2. Declarative
3. Exclamatory
4. Imperative
5. Declarative
6. Declarative
7. Interrogative
8. Exclamatory
9. Exclamatory
10. Declarative

BASIC PUNCTUATION MARKS

It goes without saying that sentences need punctuation to help them to make sense. Let's revise the main punctuation marks: the capital letter, full stop, question mark and exclamation mark.

CAPITAL LETTER

Your aim is to be ABLE to PRINT capital letters in the right place, so think of **ABLE PRINTS:**

A	Abbreviations (e.g. UK for United Kingdom)
B	Beginning of a sentence
L	Languages (e.g. French, English, Spanish)
E	Emphasising words (e.g. BANG!)
P	Places, and words relating to them (e.g. Africa, African)
R	Religions (e.g. Christianity, Buddhism)
I	I – always talk about yourself with a capital letter
N	Names of people, places, countries, organisations, days and months
T	Titles of books and films (first letter and the important words only e.g. *Of Mice and Men*)
S	Special days (e.g. Christmas Eve)

Important Note!

People often use capital letters in an informal way to emphasise words. I wouldn't do this in an English lesson or exam because your writing should be formal. Compare:

Informal: The door shut. BANG!
Formal: The door shut with a bang.   OR   The door banged shut.

Always think about how you can rewrite capitalised word(s) to make your sentences more formal.

FULL STOP

Here are the rules for full stops:
1. They go at the end of declarative sentences (statements) and some imperatives.
2. They're also in website and email addresses: http://www.mrbruff.com/ or info@mrbruff.com
3. They are used with some abbreviations, for example: a.m. p.m. e.g. i.e. Feb.
4. In American English, they're used after Mr, Mrs and Miss.

QUESTION MARK

A question mark ends an interrogative sentence (a direct question). For example: Are you doing your GCSEs?

There's never a full stop after a question mark because it has one already.

EXCLAMATION MARK

1. Use an exclamation mark at the end of an exclamatory sentence (exclamation) to show surprise, a strong emotion or pain. Sometimes, it shows that you're speaking more loudly than usual. For example: Ow! That hurt! I didn't see you! Sorry!
2. An exclamation mark sometimes ends an imperative sentence (command). For example: Look at me!

There's never a full stop after an exclamation mark because, like the question mark, it has one already. Only use **one** exclamation mark after a word. If you use two or more, this is too informal.

Test Yourself!

Read the sentences and insert the capital letters, full stops, question marks and exclamation marks in the correct place. Then check your answers on the next page.

1. i have lived in spain, ethiopia, singapore and venezuela
2. have you read 'of mice and men'
3. the history of the houses of parliament started 900 years ago with the anglo-saxons
4. some abbreviations like usa don't have full stops
5. 'i don't believe it' she exclaimed
6. i'm spending christmas at my grandparents' house in manchester
7. is anyone at home
8. fantastic see you in august
9. wednesday is ok with me
10. did you know that i e means 'that is' and e g means 'for example'

1. **I** have lived in **S**pain, **E**thiopia, **S**ingapore and **V**enezuela**.**
2. **H**ave you read '**O**f **M**ice and **M**en'**?**
3. **T**he history of the **H**ouses of **P**arliament started 900 years ago with the **A**nglo-**S**axons**.**
4. **S**ome abbreviations like **USA** don't have full stops**.**
5. '**I** don't believe it**!**' she exclaimed**.**
6. **I**'m spending **C**hristmas at my grandparents' house in **M**anchester**.**
7. **I**s anyone at home**?**
8. **F**antastic**! S**ee you in **A**ugust**!**
9. **W**ednesday is **OK** with me**.**
10. **D**id you know that i**.**e**.** means 'that is' and e**.**g**.** means 'for example'**?**

Were any of your answers different? This might be because you said them *in a particular way*. For example, these answers are exclamatory and so have an exclamation mark to show enthusiasm:

> I have lived in Spain, Ethiopia, Singapore and Venezuela!
> I'm spending Christmas at my grandparents' house in Manchester!
> Fantastic! See you in August!

However, with the next sentence, the full stop at the end shows that the speaker is speaking in a more matter-of-fact way or is simply ending a conversation. For example: Fantastic! See you in August.

Try reading the above sentences out loud. Remember that the punctuation gives you clues about how to say them.

Joke Break

An exclamation mark and a question mark are on a date. They argue.
  The exclamation mark exclaims, "Why do you always question everything?"
  The question mark replies, "Why are you always shouting at me?"

Common Mistakes

How many errors with capital letters, full stops, question marks and exclamation marks can you find and correct? Check your answers on the next page. (The speech marks, by the way, are all correct.)

1. "Stop," she yelled at the top of her voice.

2. "Why," he asked.

3. She replied, "Because I said so?"

4. "Will you forgive me!" he asked.

5. "What?!" she replied in a shocked voice.

Joke Break
SOME CAPITAL LETTERS WALKED INTO A SCHOOL.

1. "Stop!" she yelled at the top of her voice. (If you're giving an order and you have **loud** verbs such as *shout, exclaim, scream, yell, rage, bellow, roar*, etc., it's better to have an exclamation mark. There's also no capital letter after the exclamation mark because it's inside speech marks.)
2. "Why?" he asked. (For the same reason as question 1, there's no capital letter after the question mark.)
3. "Because I said so." (This is a statement, not a question, so it needs a full stop at the end. If you keep the question mark, it sounds as if the speaker is either doubtful or sarcastic.)
4. "Will you forgive me?" he asked.
5. "What?" she replied in a shocked voice. (Using a question mark and an exclamation mark together is common with texting and informal writing, but it's too informal for English lessons and exams. Use one or the other, depending on the meaning of the sentence. With the above example, *what* is a question, so it needs a question mark.

Joke Break
A question mark walked into a school?

Fascinating Fact!

There's a non-standard punctuation mark called the interrobang, which combines the question mark and exclamation mark. It looks like this:

The interrobang was invented by American Martin K. Speckter in 1962. Speckter was the president of an advertising agency, and he wanted a punctuation mark that expressed excitement and disbelief at the same time. The word interrobang comes from **interrogative** and **bang**, which is printer slang for an exclamation mark.

The interrobang was used mainly in the advertising industry, and it became fashionable in the 1960s. Some typewriter companies even put it on their typefaces. But it never caught on—nowadays, it's rarely used.

WHAT NEXT?

We'll review other punctuation marks in future chapters. Until then, how much grammar from previous English lessons do you remember?

Identify the difference between these two sentences:

A zombie chased a dog.
A dog was chased by a zombie.

Check your answer in the next chapter.

Chapter 2: The Active and Passive Voice

A zombie chased a dog.
A dog was chased by a zombie.

All sentences are written in the active or passive voice; in other words, they're either active sentences or passive sentences. The first sentence in the above example is about what the zombie is doing. This makes the zombie the subject, so the sentence is active. In the second sentence, the focus is on the unfortunate dog, which is the object of the sentence. If we wanted to, we could delete *a zombie* to focus even more on the object being chased—the dog.

But how do we recognise subjects and objects? Why is this useful? Let's start with the grammar, and then we'll explore how it all fits together.

ACTIVE SENTENCES: SUBJECT + VERB

Read this sentence: *She eats.* Now study the table:

Question	Answer	Therefore...
Who eats?	*She*	*She* is the subject of the sentence
What does she do?	*eats*	*eats* is the verb

We'll look at verbs in more detail in the next chapter. For the moment, let's remember that most of them are *doing words*. **In active sentences, the subject always *does* the verb.**

Test Yourself!

Read the sentences below and label the subjects and verbs. There will be some words left over—just ignore them for the moment. Check your answers on the next page.

1. The dog chased the ball.

2. The child ate all the sweets.

3. She weeded the garden.

4. I broke my pen.

5. They walked to the cinema.

6. We missed the bus.

7. He arrived late.

8. She only drinks water.

9. The cat drank its milk.

10. The wind blew the hat off his head.

Joke Break
An active sentence walked into a school.

---

1. The dog chased the ball. (The dog – SUBJECT, chased – VERB)
2. The child ate all the sweets. (The child – SUBJECT, ate – VERB)
3. She weeded the garden. (She – SUBJECT, weeded – VERB)
4. I broke my pen. (I – SUBJECT, broke – VERB)
5. They walked to the cinema. (They – SUBJECT, walked – VERB)
6. We missed the bus. (We – SUBJECT, missed – VERB)
7. He arrived late. (He – SUBJECT, arrived – VERB)
8. She only drinks water. (She – SUBJECT, drinks – VERB)
9. The cat drank its milk. (The cat – SUBJECT, drank – VERB)
10. The wind blew the hat off his head. (The wind – SUBJECT, blew – VERB)

WHY DO I NEED TO KNOW ABOUT ACTIVE SENTENCES?

Active sentences are dynamic. They speak of action. They make you sound firm, decisive and strong. There's no messing around with this sentence type.

Let's examine them in action. The following extract is from *The Picture of Dorian Gray* by Oscar Wilde. Dorian Gray describes his love for Sibyl Vane, a young actress who is playing the part of Juliet in *Romeo and Juliet.* The active sentences add passion and strength to his feelings:

> *"She is all the great heroines of the world in one. She is more than an individual. You laugh, but I tell you she has genius. I love her, and I must make her love me. You, who know all the secrets of life, tell me how to charm Sibyl Vane to love me! I want to make Romeo jealous. I want the dead lovers of the world to hear our laughter and grow sad. I want a breath of our passion to stir their dust into consciousness, to wake their ashes into pain. My God, Harry, how I worship her!"*
>
> *He was walking up and down the room as he spoke. Hectic spots of red burned on his cheeks. He was terribly excited.*

OBJECTS

Now that we know how to identify subjects and verbs, it's time to look at objects. Objects receive the action of a verb. Read this sentence: *The dog chased the ball.* Now study the table:

Question	Answer	Therefore...
Who chased?	*The dog*	*The dog* is the subject.
What did he do?	*chased*	*chased* is the verb.
What did he chase?	*the ball*	*the ball* is the object.

Label the subject, verb and object in each sentence. Then check your answers on the next page.

1. She ate pasta.

2. He entered the room.

3. The dog chewed a bone.

4. They went home.

5. The cat sat on the mat.

1. She ate pasta. (She – SUBJECT, ate – VERB, pasta – OBJECT)
2. He entered the room. (He – SUBJECT, entered – VERB, the room – OBJECT)
3. The dog chewed a bone. (The dog – SUBJECT, chewed – VERB, a bone – OBJECT)
4. They went home. (They – SUBJECT, went – VERB, home – OBJECT)
5. The cat sat on the mat. (The cat – SUBJECT, sat – VERB, the mat – OBJECT)

PASSIVE SENTENCES EXPLAINED

Passive sentences always focus on the **object** of a sentence. Compare:

- He sliced some bread. (Active: subject, verb, object)
- Some bread was sliced by him. (Passive: object, verb, subject)

With passive sentences, alter the verb and add the word *by* if you choose to keep the subject. In fact, the subject becomes so unimportant that you could leave it out altogether. For example: Some bread was sliced.

Test Yourself!

Turn the active sentences below into passive sentences. Remember that you'll have to alter some of the verbs. Put brackets around words you could leave out. For example:

I sat on a chair. → A chair was sat on (by me).

1. I wrote an essay.

2. He climbed the tree.

3. She ate an apple.

4. We entered the room.

5. The gang raided the shop.

Check your answers on the next page.

Fascinating Fact!
When we speak, we mostly use active sentences. It would be normal, for example, to say: *I love her.* However, it would sound odd to use the passive: *She is loved by me.*

Fascinating Fact!
If you're not sure whether a sentence is active or passive, try the **zombie test**: if you can add *by zombies* after a verb and the sentence makes sense, it is probably passive. If it doesn't make sense, it's likely to be active. For example: The dog was chased **by zombies**. (This makes sense, so it's passive.)   Zombies chased **by zombies** her. (This does not make sense, so it's active.)   This doesn't work all the time, but it's a good general guideline.

1. An essay was written (by me).
2. The tree was climbed (by him).
3. An apple was eaten (by her).
4. The room was entered (by us).
5. The shop was raided (by the gang).

WHEN DO WE USE PASSIVE SENTENCES?

To Emphasise the object

There's a well-known story that in 1897 the American author Mark Twain was in London when he heard that his obituary (a notice of his death) had been published. He sent a telegram to America, which said: *The reports of my death are greatly exaggerated.* Obviously, *reports of my death* is the object. The fact that he uses the word *my* is unexpected and adds humour, emphasising that he is alive.

To be deliberately vague

Use passive sentences when you want to be deliberately vague about a subject. For example, imagine you're a politician who's just done something so bad that it's in the news. You don't want to admit that you've made a mistake, so what could you say? *Mistakes were made.* Now you're not blaming anyone, or even taking any responsibility!

In reports

Scientific reports always used to be written in the passive voice. For example: *The gas was collected in a test tube.* Why? Because the experiment was more important than the person recording it.

Times are a-changing, however, and nowadays the active voice is more common when recording scientific experiments. Today, this is more normal: *We collected the gas in a test tube.* Isn't it lovely to know that you, the subject of the sentence, have become more important in science?

Joke Break
A school was walked into by a passive sentence.

WHAT NEXT?

You should now understand:

- The parts of a sentence: subject, verb, object
- The active voice
- The passive voice

You'll be building on this knowledge of grammar in future chapters. Before we finish, let's test your knowledge. Can you identify, explain and correct these common mistakes?

Common Mistakes

Find the mistakes in these sentences. Then check your answers on the next page.

1. I was sat in the garden, reading a book.

2. I cut my hair yesterday.

1. **I was sat in the garden, reading a book.**

The correct answer is: *I was sitting in the garden, reading a book.* The subject is *I* and—at that particular moment in time—*was sitting* and *reading* are unfinished, continuous actions (see chapter 7, past continuous tense). The *I* is in control of the action of sitting and reading. This should therefore be an active sentence.

The incorrect example is a passive sentence. The *I* is the passive object of the sentence. It's almost as if an adult sat the speaker (a young child, perhaps) in the garden whilst the child was reading a book.

2. **I cut my hair yesterday.**

The correct answer is: *I had my hair cut yesterday.* The word *had* shows that another person did this. You are the object, and this should be a passive sentence. The hairdresser cut your hair—not you.

If you are an incredibly talented hairdresser, able to give yourself a fabulous haircut, ignore this explanation.

Fascinating Fact!

Sometimes, a sentence can have two objects. Example:
> **ACTIVE:** Millie lent a **science book** to **Tom**.
> **PASSIVE:** **A science book** was lent to **Tom** by Millie.

WHAT NEXT?

Millie, book and *hairdresser* are all nouns, the subject of the next chapter.

First, however, let's finish this chapter with a joke:

Joke Break

The Three Voices in Writing

1. Active Voice:
> You ate all the chocolate.

2. Passive Voice:
> All the chocolate was eaten (by you).

3. Passive-Aggressive Voice:
> You ate all the chocolate, but don't worry about that. I'm fine with it. I didn't want any, despite oversleeping, missing breakfast and dying with hunger all morning. You knew I'd been looking forward to break time when I could eat it, but you obviously needed it more than me.

Chapter 3: Nouns

Teacher:	**Harry, give me a sentence that begins with 'I'.**
Harry:	**I is—**
Teacher:	**No, Harry! It's *I am...***
Harry:	**OK! *I am* the ninth letter of the alphabet.**

Imagine that grammar is made of bricks. Each brick is a chunk of language that does something different. These bricks are called parts of speech, and there are nine of them. As you can see in the joke, they must fit together properly in order to make sense. In this chapter, we'll review and extend your knowledge of the part of speech called nouns.

WHAT'S A NOUN?

A noun is the name of a thing. When you have one thing (for example, *a pen*), it's a singular noun. When there are two or more, you make a plural by adding *–s* (for example, *pen<u>s</u>*). Most plural nouns end with *–s*, but there are exceptions.

To understand the spelling rules, we need to remember that vowels are the letters A, E, I, O, U and consonants are all the other letters. (Interestingly, some people count the letter Y as a vowel.)

Test Yourself! Irregular Spelling of Plural Nouns

Can you work out the spelling rules for making words plural? Some of the nouns in the chart below follow the rule of adding *–s*, but others don't. **Read the words aloud and use your knowledge of vowels and consonants to work out the rules and complete the chart.** Answer the question for column two. Then study the example plural form and write the spelling rule in the last column. The first two have been done for you. Check your answers on the next page.

Example Singular Noun	What's special about the Singular Noun?	Example Plural Noun	Spelling Rule
story	consonant plus *–y*	stories	change -y to -ies
storey	vowel plus -y	storeys	add *–s* as normal
wolf		wolves	
life		lives	
cliff		cliffs	
witch, glass wish, fox		witches, glasses wishes, foxes	
quiz		quizzes	
fee		fees	
cactus		cacti	

Example Singular Noun	What's special about the Singular Noun?	Example Plural Noun	Spelling Rule
story	consonant plus –y	stories	change -y to -ies
storey	vowel plus -y	storeys	add –s as normal
wolf	ends in -f	wolves	change -f to -ves
life	ends in –fe	lives	change –fe to –ves
cliff	ends in -ff	cliffs	add –s as normal
witch, glass wish, fox	end in-ch, -s, -sh, or -x	witches, glasses wishes, foxes	add –es
quiz	ends in -z	quizzes	double the –z and add -es
fee	*ends in a double vowel*	fees	add –s as normal
cactus	ends in -us	cacti	-us changes to -i. NB: *cactuses* is becoming more acceptable.

Test Yourself! Nouns ending in –o

Many nouns end in –o. Unfortunately, there's no rule for which ones take –s or –es in their plural form. Use your dictionary to find the plural forms of the words below, and then write them in the correct column. Check your answers on the next page.

Singular noun:

Tomato   zero   biro   hero   toe   studio   potato   volcano   kilo   piano

Plural of nouns ending in -o

-s	-es

-s	-es
Zeros	Tomatoes
Biros	Heroes
Toes	Potatoes
Studios	Volcanoes
Kilos	
Pianos	

Joke Break

Ken the cactus and Katie the cactus are arguing.

Ken: You need to think about both of us. Remember, it's cact-*us*!

Katie: Actually, the plural is cact-*i*.

IRREGULAR PLURAL WORDS

Some words are Anglo-Saxon in origin and don't follow any rules at all. These are called irregular plurals. Here are some examples:

man → men   child → children   mouse → mice

woman → women   foot → feet   person → people

Other nouns don't change at all when they become plural. For example: deer, fish, sheep, offspring, series and species.

Fascinating fact!

After the Vikings invaded, we began to add –s to make plurals.

Test Yourself!

Read the sentences below. Put the noun in brackets in its plural form. Some are irregular plurals, so be careful!

1.   I have _____(pencil) and two pencil _____(sharpener) on my desk.

2.   That man has had four _____(wife)!

3.   How many _____(box) are in your car?

4.   A shirt has a collar and two _____(cuff).

5.   My school has two art _____(studio).

6.   I like doing _____(quiz).

7.   Every Sunday, my friend and I go to different _____(church).

8.   I like autumn when _____(leaf) fall from the _____(tree).

9.   I don't like _____(kiss) very much.

10. We sold all the_____(sheep)!

18

Now check your answers.

1. I have <u>pencils</u> and two pencil <u>sharpeners</u> on my desk.
2. That man has had four <u>wives</u>!
3. How many <u>boxes</u> are in your car?
4. A shirt has a collar and two <u>cuffs</u>.
5. My school has two art <u>studios</u>.
6. I like doing <u>quizzes</u>.
7. Every Sunday, my friend and I go to different <u>churches</u>.
8. I like autumn when <u>leaves</u> fall from the <u>trees</u>.
9. I don't like <u>kisses</u> very much.
10. We sold all the <u>sheep</u>!

Fascinating Fact!

Some words take two plural forms. For example, *hoof* can be *hoofs* and also *hooves*.

SPELLING TIP!

When a teacher—of any subject—returns your work to you, note any spelling mistakes. Then write the corrections in a spelling log. Learn at least one correction a day.

CONCRETE, ABSTRACT, PROPER AND COLLECTIVE NOUNS

There are four types of noun:

Type of Noun	Definition	Examples
Concrete Noun	Things that you can touch (like concrete), see, smell, hear or taste.	chair, keyboard, money, water
Abstract Noun	Things that you cannot touch, see, smell, hear or taste.	beauty, love, anger, freedom, bravery
Proper Nouns	The <u>name</u> of a specific person, place, organisation or thing. They always begin with a capital letter.	Jim Smith, Swansea, Buckingham Palace, the Statue of Liberty
Collective Noun	A group of things, people or animals.	an anthology of poems a choir of students a gaggle of geese

---

Fascinating Fact!

A baby's first words are nouns.

Fascinating Fact!

There's no collective noun for koala bears because they're solitary creatures and don't move around in groups.

COMPOUND NOUNS

Two or more nouns joined together make a compound noun. Some are joined with a hyphen and others are one word. For example: hosepipe, football, sister-in-law and stepfather.

A hyphen sometimes makes a compound noun easier to understand. For example, we need the hyphen with *ice-cream*. If it's not there, your reader might think that you are talking about *an ice cream* i.e. cream made of ice!

Fascinating Fact!

Many compound nouns have evolved over time. For example, a firefly used to be spelt as two words: *fire fly*. It then became *fire-fly* and finally *firefly*. You might notice more examples when you are reading 19th-century fiction and nonfiction.

WHY DO I NEED TO KNOW ABOUT NOUNS?

They show off your vocabulary

Collective nouns are great for showcasing your range of vocabulary. Let's see how much you know.

Test Yourself!

Match the collective nouns below. The first one has been done for you.

1. A class of	a. people
2. An eloquence of	b. musicians
3. A crowd of	c. students
4. A board of	d. lawyers
5. A murder of	e. lions
6. A coven of	f. elephants
7. A prickle of	g. sheep
8. An orchestra of	h. kittens
9. A colony of	i. crows
10. A flock of	j. witches
11. A herd of	k. bees
12. A school of	l. directors
13. A pride of	m. hedgehogs
14. A swarm of	n. fish
15. A kindle of	o. ants

Joke Break

A robin and a pigeon are admiring some flowers in a park. Suddenly, they see a large eagle with a sharp dagger slowly advancing towards two oblivious crows, which are busy eating worms.

The robin turns to his friend the pigeon and asks, "What's happening?"

"Oh, dear," the pigeon replies. "It looks like a murder of crows."

1. C	6. j	11. f
2. d	7. m	12. n
3. a	8. b	13. e.
4. l	9. o	14. k.
5. i	10. g	15. h

They can help your analytical skills

When you're reading, look for interesting nouns to analyse. In this extract from *The Moonstone* by Wilkie Collins, the narrator asks Mr. Betteredge to write down the story of a stolen diamond:

> *"In this matter of the Diamond," he said, "the characters of innocent people have suffered under suspicion already—as you know. The memories of innocent people may suffer, hereafter, for want of a record of the facts to which those who come after us can appeal. There can be no doubt that this strange family story of ours ought to be told. And I think, Betteredge, Mr. Bruff and I together have hit on the right way of telling it."*

The concrete noun 'Diamond' looks odd, as it has been capitalised to become a proper noun, emphasising its importance to the characters and story.

The abstract nouns 'characters' (meaning reputations) and 'suspicion' and 'memories' set the tone of an enquiry—*The Moonstone* is, after all, believed to be the first ever detective novel in English!

The proper noun 'Mr Bruff' adds weight to the speaker's request. The reader senses that the speaker has ganged up with Mr. Bruff behind the scenes to persuade Mr. Betteredge to write his version of the story.

Of course, you don't have to label the nouns: your analysis is far more important. But terminology can add weight to what you say.

NOUN PHRASES

A noun phrase is a word or a group of words that describes a noun to make it more interesting. It might be a short phrase of just two words: *my cat*. Or it might contain a little more description: *my oldest cat*. Or it might be longer: *my oldest cat with one eye*.

The descriptive words can come before (premodify) or after (postmodify) a noun or, as we saw with the most recent example, both. These examples are all noun phrases to describe the noun *cat*:

Premodified Noun Phrases	Postmodified Noun phrases
my cat	cat on the fence
my oldest cat	cat in the garden
both of my cats	cat hissing at me
my four cats	cat purring over there
all of my four cats	cat that ran away
my gorgeous cat	cat that bit me
my purring, fluffy, flea-bitten cat	cat with a red collar in the garden drinking milk.

EXAMPLE NOUN PHRASES IN LITERATURE

Bleak House

In this extract from *Bleak House*, Charles Dickens uses noun phrases to create a strong, visual and atmospheric picture of the setting.

Sometimes, there is more than one noun in a noun phrase, so always ask yourself which noun is the most important—this is the *main noun*. Don't attempt to find and analyse all of the noun phrases in an extract—just choose the most interesting ones.

> *Fog everywhere. Fog up the river, where it flows among green aits and meadows; fog down the river, where it rolls defiled among the tiers of shipping and the waterside pollutions of a great (and dirty) city. Fog on the Essex marshes, fog on the Kentish heights. Fog creeping into the cabooses of collier-brigs; fog lying out on the yards and hovering in the rigging of great ships; fog drooping on the gunwales of barges and small boats. Fog in the eyes and throats of ancient Greenwich pensioners, wheezing by the firesides of their wards; fog in the stem and bowl of the afternoon pipe of the wrathful skipper, down in his close cabin; fog cruelly pinching the toes and fingers of his shivering little 'prentice boy on deck. Chance people on the bridges peeping over the parapets into a nether sky of fog, with fog all round them, as if they were up in a balloon and hanging in the misty clouds.*

The noun phrases develop the idea of being invaded by fog, creating a cold, hostile atmosphere. The repetition of the main noun 'fog' emphasises the extent of the fog, which cannot be stopped.

A Christmas Carol

Now read this extract from *A Christmas Carol* by Charles Dickens. Scrooge has been disconcerted by the face of his dead business partner appearing on his door knocker. He now decides to check his house:

> *Sitting-room, bedroom, lumber-room. All as they should be. Nobody under the table, nobody under the sofa; a small fire in the grate; spoon and basin ready; and the little saucepan of gruel (Scrooge had a cold in his head) upon the hob. Nobody under the bed; nobody in the closet; nobody in his dressing gown, which was hanging up in a suspicious attitude against the wall. Lumber-room as usual. Old fire-guard, old shoes, two fish baskets, washing-stand on three legs, and a poker.*

The underlined noun phrases build momentum as he checks his house for anything out of the ordinary. We can almost hear Scrooge saying these words out loud, perhaps reassuring himself as he methodically checks everything. Then Dickens deliberately positions the final noun phrase 'and a poker' at the end of the paragraph. By drawing the reader's attention to this, we have a hint that Scrooge is worried and perhaps reassured to have a potential weapon for protection.

WHAT NEXT?

You've revised the spelling of irregular plural nouns, reviewed the categories of nouns and examined noun phrases. Before we review the next part of speech, let's finish this chapter with a...

> **Joke Break**
> It's only a murder of crows if there's probable caws.

Chapter 4: Determiners

There's a currently a fashion for teenagers to make deliberate mistakes with grammar. They speak *teen slang* in order to fit in with their friends:

> **What's, like, so wrong with it? Especially, like, when it's sort of used to show I'm thinking about stuff and that's good, innit? Many people are like, "I can talk how I want. Don't, like, sort of, tell me how to talk!"**

If you speak teen slang, I agree that it's not my place to tell you how to speak. My point is that—in an English exam—if you write the way you speak, you're likely to lose marks. After your exams, you might want to apply for an apprenticeship, a university place, or look for a job. If you have an interview (and the job involves talking to the public) teen slang could work against you.

We're not asking you to change who you are. However, you need to be able to switch between informal and standard English. You need to use verbs instead of the word *like*, and you also need to use determiners correctly. In this chapter, we'll quickly revise what determiners are, and then we'll focus on common mistakes.

WHAT'S A DETERMINER?

A determiner introduces a noun, and it tells you whether it is particular or general. For example: *a* cat, *my* cat, *some* cats.

> **Fascinating Fact!**
>
> The above examples are noun phrases—you can make noun phrases with determiners!

Here are some more examples of determiners:

Type	Examples
Articles	a, an, the
Demonstratives	this, that, these, those
Numbers	One, two, three
Ordinal numbers	First, second, third
Possessive adjectives	My, your, his, her, its, our, their
Quantifiers	Some, any, much, many, little, few, more, less

COMMON MISTAKES: ARTICLES

In the following extract, there are three errors. How many can you find? Underline and correct them:

> I was talking to this man, who told me about this new computer. It has a internet wireless connection guaranteed anywhere in the world.

I was talking to <u>a</u> man, who told me about <u>a</u> computer. It has <u>an</u> internet wireless connection guaranteed anywhere in the world.

The words *a* or *an* are the **indefinite article**. We use them the first time we talk about something or someone.

When does *a* change to *an*?

The indefinite article *a* changes to *an* before words that begin with a vowel sound. Examples: *an apple, an elephant, an interest, an orange, an umbrella.*

Notice that I said vowel *sound* because you ignore the spelling! For example, you don't pronounce the -*h* in hour. The beginning of the word sounds like the vowel *a*- so you say an hour.

There are other exceptions—again, think about how you say words. You wouldn't say *an* one-bedroom house. The -*o* is a vowel but it doesn't *sound* like one. It sounds like a -*w* so we say *a* one-bedroom house.

The

The is called the **definite article** because we are definite that we know who or what we're talking about. It might be...
- Someone so well-known that we already know who they are. Examples: the head of English at your school, the government, or the pope.
- A thing that everyone knows about. Examples: the sun, the M25, or the science block in your school.
- Someone or something that you've mentioned once; the second time, we now know who or what you're talking about. For example: I picked up *a* phone. *The* phone was broken.
- With plural nouns. You can't say *a ears*, but you can say *the ears*.

Test Yourself!

Twelve Years a Slave by Solomon Northup is the true story of how he was kidnapped in 1841 and then sold into slavery. In this extract from his autobiography, Northup wakes and describes his surroundings. Read the extract and insert *a, an* or *the* in the right place.

At length I heard _____(1) crowing of a cock, and soon _____ (2) distant rumbling sound, as of carriages hurrying through _____ (3) streets, came to my ears, and I knew that it was day. No ray of light, however, penetrated my prison. Finally, I heard footsteps immediately overhead, as of some one walking to and fro. It occurred to me then that I must be in _____(4) underground apartment, and _____(5) damp, mouldy odors* of _____ (6) place confirmed the supposition. _____ (7) noise above continued for at least _____ (8) hour, when, at last, I heard footsteps approaching from without. _____ (9) key rattled in the lock— _____ (10) strong door swung back upon its hinges...

**Note the American spelling of odours.*

> *At length I heard <u>the (1)</u> crowing of a cock, and soon <u>a (2)</u> distant rumbling sound, as of carriages hurrying through <u>the (3)</u> streets, came to my ears, and I knew that it was day. No ray of light, however, penetrated my prison. Finally, I heard footsteps immediately overhead, as of some one walking to and fro. It occurred to me then that I must be in <u>an (4)</u> underground apartment, and <u>the (5)</u> damp, mouldy odors of <u>the (6)</u> place confirmed the supposition. <u>The (7)</u> noise above continued for at least <u>an (8)</u> hour, when, at last, I heard footsteps approaching from without. <u>A (9)</u> key rattled in the lock—<u>a (10)</u> strong door swung back upon its hinges...*

1. Everyone knows about the cockerel because they can all hear it.
2. It's the first time he hears this particular sound.
3. *The* is used with a plural noun.
4. *An* because 'underground' begins with a vowel sound. It's also the first time he talks about the apartment.
5. *The* is used with a plural noun.
6. He knows about the place because he's been there for a long time.
7. He has already described the noises of the cockerel, carriages and footsteps. 'The noise' links back to these.
8. *An* before *hour*, which begins with the vowel sound *a*. It's also his first reference to time.
9. The first time he talks about the key.
10. The first time he talks about the door.

Fascinating Fact!

Have you ever heard anyone say *an hotel*? This is because it's a French word, and people used to pronounce it the French way without the *-h*. Although some people still say *an hotel* today, the more popular *a hotel* is also correct.

Common Mistakes: Less/Fewer

Some people make mistakes when using *less* and *fewer*. We use *fewer* with plural countable nouns and *less* with uncountable nouns:

- **Countable nouns** are any nouns that you can count, so you can make them plural. Examples: *boy* (plural: *boys*), *chair* (plural: *chairs*), *keyboard* (plural: *keyboards*).
- **Uncountable nouns** are nouns that you can't count, and they don't have a plural form. Examples: *money, water, sugar.* It might sound odd that we can't count these items—especially money! We count coins and pounds, but we have *bags, wallets* or *purses* (countable) of money. We also have *glasses* or *bottles* (countable) of water and *spoons* (countable) of sugar.

Exceptions:
- *Less* can be used with **time**. Example: *My relationship with my boyfriend lasted less than five weeks.* You can count weeks, so you expect to use *fewer*; however, we're actually talking about **a block of time** and time is uncountable. Therefore, we say *less*.
- *Less* can also be used with **money** and **distance**. For example: *I have less than £2 in my pocket*; however, in less than three miles, I'll finish the marathon.*

Read the sentences below, fill in the gaps, and then check your answers.

1. Sorry, I can't go out tonight. I have _____ than £5 to spend.

2. _____ people went to the party than we expected.

3. Although I have _____ GCSEs than you, I have more common sense.

4. I have _____ time than I thought.

5. We have _____ than four months before our exams.

6. The _____ mistakes I make, the better my mark!

7. I need to drink _____coffee.

8. However, I drink _____ cups of coffee than you!

9. More time, _____ haste!

10. I was standing _____ than one metre away from the tiger.

Answers

1. Sorry, I can't go out tonight. I have <u>less</u> than £5 to spend.
2. <u>Fewer</u> people went to the party than we expected.
3. Although I have <u>fewer</u> GCSEs than you, I have more common sense.
4. I have <u>less</u> time than I thought.
5. We have <u>less</u> than four months before our exams.
6. The <u>fewer</u> mistakes I make, the better my mark!
7. I need to drink <u>less</u> coffee.
8. However, I drink <u>fewer</u> cups of coffee than you!
9. More time, <u>less</u> haste!
10. I was standing <u>less</u> than one metre away from the tiger.

Fascinating Fact!

In 2008, a major supermarket chain in the UK received so many complaints about the bad grammar on its fast-track checkout notices (*10 items or less*) that it took them all down! Even though *10 items or fewer* is grammatically correct, they didn't like the sound of it, so they replaced their signs with ones that said *Up to 10 items*.

Common Mistakes: Amount/Number

We use a*mount* is with uncountable nouns and *number* is with countable plural nouns.

When *number* means *some*, it takes the plural verb. For example: *A number of students are waiting for their exam results.*

When you use *the number*, it takes the singular verb. For example: *The number of students increases every year.*

Test Yourself!

Read the sentences below, fill in the gaps with *amount* or *number* and then check your answers.

1. I have a huge _____ of homework to do!

2. Why don't I want to go out with you? Well, there are a _____ of reasons.

3. There are a _____ of cute rabbits in that cage.

4. She had the right _____ of relevant experience for the job.

5. We are worried by the _____ of violence in the city centre.

6. A _____ of people want a change of government.

7. The _____ of unemployed teenagers is rising.

8. Teachers believe that a certain _____ of homework every evening is good for you.

9. Romeo and Juliet had a great _____ of love for each other.

10. The _____ of unemployed people is increasing.

Answers

1. I have a huge <u>amount</u> of homework to do! ('Homework' is an uncountable noun.)
2. Why don't I want to go out with you? Well, there are a <u>number</u> of reasons. ('a <u>number</u> of' = 'some' and therefore countable reasons)
3. There are a <u>number</u> of cute rabbits in that cage. ('a <u>number</u> of' = 'some' + countable rabbits)
4. She had the right <u>amount</u> of relevant experience for the job. ('Experience' is an uncountable noun.)
5. We are worried by the <u>amount</u> of violence in the city centre. ('Violence' is an uncountable noun.)
6. A <u>number</u> of people want a change of government. ('a <u>number</u> of' = 'some' and therefore countable people.)
7. The <u>number</u> of unemployed teenagers is rising. ('<u>The</u> number + singular verb and therefore countable teenagers)
8. Teachers believe that a certain <u>amount</u> of homework every evening is good for you. (Unsurprisingly, 'homework' is an uncountable noun.)
9. Romeo and Juliet had a great <u>amount</u> of love for each other. ('love' is an uncountable noun. Many poets have written about how it cannot be measured.)
10. The <u>number</u> of unemployed people is increasing. ('<u>The</u> number + singular verb and therefore countable unemployed people.)

Another (perhaps?) Fascinating Fact!

In 2015, Kerry Lewis, the author of this guide, went to a local supermarket and saw a queueing sign for people with '4 items or less'. She fired a series of annoyed tweets at the supermarket:

'How can we expect students to learn good grammar when they're surrounded by bad examples?'

'I can understand this with small shops who are focusing on making ends meet, but you employ people who should know better!'

The supermarket was very apologetic and asked which branch she shopped at. The next time she went there, the offending sign had been replaced with '4 items or fewer'.

Chapter 5: Interjections

Huh?

Our next part of speech is the interjection. I always feel sorry for interjections—grammatically, they're quite lonely little things. They're not related to other parts of a sentence and, if you delete them, your sentence will still make perfect grammatical sense. By way of example, read this conversation about interjections:

Person A: If they don't add anything to the grammar, why do we have them?

Person B: Well, they express sudden feelings and emotions. Yes! Think enthusiasm, excitement, happiness, surprise, horror, disgust…

Person A: Hey! I've just realised that we don't need interjections. Oh! We could get rid of them completely!

Person B: Duh, it wouldn't be the same. We *need* to express strong feelings and emotions! Good grief! We're people, not robots!

Person A: Ahem, it's worth knowing that not all interjections are used with exclamation marks. Hmm, some interjections sound like sounds.

Person B: Phew, that's worth knowing! Yea!

PUNCTUATION WITH INTERJECTIONS

Unless it's an exclamation, we separate interjections with a comma.

Test Yourself!

There are ten interjections in the above conversation. Underline them and then check your answers on the next page.

Joke Break

The daughter of a Neanderthal (caveman) is chatting to her friend.

She says, "My father is a man of few words. He only communicates with nouns and interjections."

Person A: If they don't add anything to the grammar, why do we have them?

Person B: Well, they express sudden feelings and emotions. Yes! Think enthusiasm, excitement, happiness, surprise, horror, disgust…

Person A: Hey! I've just realised that we don't need interjections. Oh! We could get rid of them completely!

Person B: Duh, it wouldn't be the same. We *need* to express strong feelings and emotions! Good grief! We're people, not robots!

Person A: Ahem, it's worth knowing that not all interjections are used with exclamation marks. Hmm, some interjections sound like sounds.

Person B: Phew, that's worth knowing! Yea!

Fascinating Fact!

We'll now take a short pause to examine how interjections can be used in poetry.

In *Sonnet 116,* Shakespeare defines love:

> *Oh no! It is an ever-fixed mark*
> *That looks on tempests, and is never shaken*

The 'ever-fixed mark' is a lighthouse ('fixed' was pronounced *fix–id*, with two syllables, by the way). Shakespeare is saying that troubles can't shake love just as storms ('tempests') can't shake a lighthouse.

These lines are written in iambic pentameter: ten beats per line with alternating unstressed and stressed syllables. (Saying this, he sometimes added or subtracted an extra syllable or two, depending on the mood of the poem.)

If you're a budding poet, here's a handy tip: interjections are useful for making up the number of beats per line. With *Sonnet 16*, the interjection 'Oh no!' makes the beats add up to ten.

Before your teacher faints with shock, never write this in an exam! You need to analyse the poet's use of the interjection. With this particular example, the stress on 'Oh no!' emphasises Shakespeare's absolute conviction that he is right.

WHAT NEXT?

Either compete with a friend to find at least two hundred interjections on the internet or turn to the next chapter. The word 'turn' is a verb, by the way. It's our next part of speech.

Chapter 6: Verbs

Three verbs walked into a school. They chatted. They worked. They left.

WHAT'S A VERB?

There are three types of verb, and most of them, as we saw in chapter 2, are *doing* words, which we call **main verbs**. For example: *The trees creak in the violent storm*. What do the trees do? The answer is *creak*. Therefore, *creak* is a **main verb**.

Here's a summary and explanation of the three categories of verbs:

	Main Verb	**Auxiliary Verb**	**Modal verb**
Definition:	An action or 'doing' word.	Helps the main verb.	Shows that something is certain or possible.
Example verbs:	Most verbs	*do, have, be*	*can, could, would, may, might, will, must, may, shall, should, ought to*
Example sentence:	Jemma *finishes* her homework.	*Did* Jemma finish her homework? She *has* finished her homework. It *is* done!	Jemma *might* finish her homework.

Test Yourself!

Underline and label the main, auxiliary and modal verbs in the sentences below. Then check your answers on the next page.

1. She eats her five portions of fruit or vegetables a day.
2. He exercises regularly.
3. He is going home.
4. She might go to the cinema.
5. He works every Saturday.
6. Did they play tennis?
7. She has gone.
8. May I leave the table?
9. I have just drunk some water.
10. He could be late.

Fascinating Fact!

Sometimes *to be* and *to have* do not help other verbs. For example: She *is* rich. Because it's no longer a helping auxiliary verb, *to be* becomes an **intransitive verb,** a verb with no direct object. However, *have* has a direct object (e.g. I *have* lots of money), so it is classified as a **transitive verb**.

1. She <u>eats</u> **(main)** her five portions of fruit or vegetables a day.
2. He <u>exercises</u> **(main)** regularly.
3. He <u>is</u> **(auxiliary)** <u>going</u> **(main)** home.
4. She <u>might</u> **(modal)** <u>go</u> **(main)** to the cinema.
5. He <u>works</u> **(main)** every Saturday.
6. <u>Did</u> **(auxiliary)** they <u>play</u> **(main)** tennis?
7. She <u>has</u> **(auxiliary)** <u>gone</u> **(main)**.
8. <u>May</u> **(modal)** I <u>leave</u> **(main)** the table?
9. I <u>have</u> **(auxiliary)** just <u>drunk</u> **(main)** some water.
10. He <u>could</u> **(modal)** <u>be</u> **(intransitive)** late.

With the last example, the modal verb *could* helps *be*. Did you read the *Fascinating Fact* on the previous page?

SUBJECT AND VERB AGREEMENT

In chapter 2, we saw that the subject of a sentence is who or what the sentence is about. The subject and verb must always agree with each other—in other words, they must make sense.

Test Yourself!

Underline the correct verb in brackets. Then check your answers on the next page.

1. I (was / were) late.

2. Both of us (is / are) French.

3. You (was / were) a long time.

4. Everybody (has / have) a favourite subject.

5. He (was / were) reading a newspaper.

6. Neither of us (has / have) any money.

7. We (was / were) walking down the street.

8. There (was / were) only two ways to do this.

9. Neither my sisters nor my dad (likes / like) Brussel sprouts.

10. Neither my dad nor my sisters (likes / like) Brussel sprouts.

Fascinating Fact!

There are three basic tenses: the present tense, the past tense and the future tense.

These can be subdivided into verb tenses, depending on what you want to say. For example, *When I was at school, I <u>walked</u> home every day* is a regular action (so it's in the simple past tense). *However, I <u>was walking</u> home at 3.30 p.m.* describes an unfinished action (so it's in the past continuous tense).

If you're interested in reading about the verb tenses, they are summarised in the next chapter.

---

1. I <u>was</u> late.
2. Both of us <u>are</u> French. (This is another way of saying *we are*)
3. You <u>were </u>a long time.
4. Everybody <u>has</u> a favourite subject. (*Body* is singular, so it's the same as saying *each person* has…)
5. He <u>was</u> reading a newspaper.
6. Neither of us <u>has </u>any money. (It's the same as saying *not one of us has…*)
7. We <u>were</u> walking down the street.
8. There <u>were</u> only two ways to do this.
9. Neither my sisters nor my **dad** <u>likes</u> Brussel sprouts. (Verb agrees with the **nearest subject noun.**)
10. Neither my dad nor my **sisters** <u>like</u> Brussel sprouts. (Verb agrees with the **nearest subject noun.**)

TENSES

When you're writing, choose a tense and stick to it. Don't mix tenses unless it's for a deliberate reason—for example, a flashback.

Spelling Rules: Simple Past Tense and Present Participles

Most verbs are regular, so you add *–ed* to form the simple past tense. Example: *Yesterday, I walked home.* To form a present participle, add *–ing.* This shows that something is <u>unfinished</u> in the past, present or future. For example:

> I was eat<u>ing</u> a sandwich yesterday when the phone rang. (Unfinished action in the PAST)
> At the moment, I am typ<u>ing</u> these rules. (Unfinished action in the PRESENT)
> This time tomorrow, I'll be sunbath<u>ing</u> on a Greek island. (Unfinished action in the FUTURE)

Sometimes you have to tweak the spelling a little. Study the chart of spelling rules below. **Read the words out loud, noting which syllables are stressed.** Then, **using your knowledge of vowels and consonants,** write the reason for each rule in the last column. The first two have been done for you.

Example Verb	Past Tense	Present Participle	Spelling Rule	Why?
love	loved	loving	drop the final *–e*	The verb ends with a silent *–e.*
free eye canoe	freed eyed canoed	freeing eyeing canoeing	keep the final *-e*	The verbs end with *-ee, -ye,* and *-oe.*
travel	travelled	travelling	double the *–l*	
beg parallel prefer stop	begged parallelled preferred stopped	begging paralleling preferring stopping	double the final consonant	
enter target	entered targeted	entering targeting	Add *-ed* and *-ing,* so why don't we double the final consonant?	
panic	panicked	panicking	add *-k*	

Example Verb	Past Tense	Present Participle	Spelling Rule	Why?
love	loved	loving	drop the final –e	The verb ends with a silent –e.
free	freed	freeing	keep the final -e	The verbs end with -ee, -ye, and -oe.
eye	eyed	eyeing		
canoe	canoed	canoeing		
travel	travelled	travelling	double the –l	The verb ends with vowel plus –l.
beg	begged	begging	double the final consonant	1. They end with a consonant & vowel & consonant. 2. <u>The stress is at end of the word</u>
parallel	parallelled	paralleling		
prefer	preferred	preferring		
stop	stopped	stopping		
enter	entered	entering	Add -ed and -ing, so why don't we double the final consonant?	1. They end with a consonant & vowel & consonant 2. <u>The stress is NOT at end of the word</u>
target	targeted	targeting		
panic	panicked	panicking	add -k	The verb ends with -c.

How did you do? If you had any wrong, I'm afraid you'll have to learn the rules. If that feels depressing, perhaps this will cheer you up:

Joke Break
Feeling tense? You must be a verb.

Fascinating Fact!
You can make noun phrases with a present participle. Examples:
the cat **hissing** at me
the cat **purring** over there

IRREGULAR VERBS

Simply add –ed to most verbs to form the simple past tense, perhaps tweaking the spelling here and there. These are called regular verbs. However, some verbs don't follow the rules, and these are called *irregular verbs*. For example: *I ate (not eated) an apple.*

Let's look at a different sentence: *I have walked twenty miles.* (In other words, I've JUST walked twenty miles, and I'm so glad it's over!) It's not a finished past event because you've only just finished it now. The verb *walked* looks as if it's in the simple past tense, but it's not. This is because it follows the auxiliary verb *have*. It's therefore called a *past participle*. You make most past participles by adding –ed, and these are regular.

Some past participles are irregular, however. For example: *I have won.* (In other words, I have JUST won.) We don't say *I have winned*, so *won* is an irregular past participle.

As a native speaker of English, you use often this grammar correctly without even thinking about it.

Or do you?

Fill in the chart of irregular verbs. The first two have been done for you. For the second column, say *Yesterday I—* and finish the sentence with the verb. In the third column, say, *I have—* and again, finish the sentence with the verb. Then check your answers.

Verb	Simple Past *(Yesterday I—)*	Past Participle *(I have—)*
Be	was You/we/they were	been
Begin	began	begun
Buy	bought	bought
Bring	brought	brought
Catch	caught	caught
Choose	chose	chosen
Come	came	come
Do	did	done
Drink	~~drunk~~ drank	drunk
Drive	drove	driven
Eat	ate	eaten
Give	gave	given
Go	went	gone
Have	had	had

Verb	Simple Past (Yesterday I—)	Past Participle (I have—)
Hide	hid	hiden
Know	knew	known
Ring	rang	rung
See	saw	seen
Show	showed	shown
Steal	stole	stolen
Take	took	taken
Tell	told	told
Think	thought	thought
Understand	understood	understood
Write	wrote	written

Fascinating Fact: Spelling of Verbs!

Generally speaking, if a verb ends in –ise, it's British English spelling while a verb ending in –ize is American spelling. For example: *analyse* is British English, and *analyze* is American English.

However, in British English, we can choose between: *organise* and *organize, realise* and *realize.* Why can we use a –z with those words? Isn't it American spelling? Well, actually, it's not!

In 1425, the first example of *organize* was recorded in the *Oxford English Dictionary* while *realize* appeared in 1611. It's an interesting fact that a verb with the -ise spelling was first recorded more than a hundred years later.

Verb	Simple Past (Yesterday I—)	Past Participle (I have—)
Be	Was / were	been
Begin	began	begun
Buy	bought	bought
Bring	brought	brought
Catch	caught	caught
Choose	chose	chosen
Come	came	come
Do	did	done
Drink	drank	drunk
Drive	drove	driven
Eat	ate	eaten
Give	gave	given
Go	went	gone
Have	had	had
Hide	hid	hidden
Know	knew	known
Ring	rang	rung
See	saw	seen
Show	showed	shown
Steal	stole	stolen
Take	took	taken
Tell	told	told
Think	thought	thought
Understand	understood	understood
Write	wrote	written

Fascinating Fact: Split Infinitives!

An infinitive is a verb before you do anything to it. For example: *to work*. If you put a word in the middle of the infinitive, it's called a split infinitive. For example, *I need to _really_ work harder.*

Some people believe that it's wrong to split an infinitive. Instead of the above example, they would write: *I _really_ need to work harder.*

Others say that this rule is a load of rubbish because it's a Latin—not English—grammar rule. Before this rule was introduced to the English language, people used to merrily split infinitives all the time.

Even today, the discussion is ongoing. So...to split or not to split? That is indeed the question. There's no right or wrong answer. To be on the safe side, avoid splitting infinitives with formal writing.

Top Tip!

When you analyse, try replacing *shows* with one of these verbs:
connotes, implies, mirrors, parallels, portrays, reveals, suggests, symbolises

Fascinating Fact: The Double Negative!

From science, you'll know that negative + negative = positive. Let's apply this to English grammar with the example sentence: *I did not do nothing.* The words *not* and *nothing* are negative words— there are two of them, so this is a double negative. Using a scientific approach, the meaning of this sentence is now positive: *I did do something!*

There's a grammar rule that we shouldn't use the double negative. In fact, using the double negative could get someone into serious trouble:

Joke Break

A man has been arrested for burglary.
> In court, the judge asks, "How do you plead?"
> The man replies, "I didn't do nothing!"
> The jury of English teachers conclude that he has just admitted his guilt.

Saying this, it's **not uncommon** to use the double negative for deliberate emphasis. It's **not unheard** of. And it's **not unknown**.

Common Mistakes with Verbs

Underline and correct the errors in the following sentences. Then check your answers on the next page.

1. I brang my mobile to school and now I've lost it! *brought*

2. I bfought some lovely clothes in the sales at the week-end.

3. If I was rich, I would buy a mansion. *were*

4. I'm going to lay down and have a nap. *lie*

5. Yes, I did it already! *have done*

6. This is great homework. I'm going to bring this book to school tomorrow. *take*

7. The true story of Solomon Northup effected me deeply. *a*

8. I should of apologised, but I didn't. *have*

9. I did not do nothing! *anything*

10. She dosent like pizza.

Joke Break
If two wrongs don't make a right, why does a double negative make a positive?

1. I <u>brought</u> (past of *bring*)
2. I <u>bought</u> (past of *bought*)
3. If I <u>were</u> (because it's a wish. See chapter 7, second conditional)
4. I'm going to <u>lie</u> down. *Lie* is often confused with *lay* (*I lay, I laid, I have laid*), which means to put someone or something down. It always has an object. For example: *They laid the table. The chicken laid an egg.*
5. If you are American, this is the correct answer. If you speak British English, it should be: *Yes, I <u>have already done it</u>!* This is called the present perfect tense (see chapter 7), which is not very common in America.
6. I'm going to <u>take</u> this book to school tomorrow. (You always *bring* things here and *take* things there.)
7. The true story of Solomon Northup <u>affected</u> me deeply. (RAVEN: Remember! Affect = Verb, Effect = Noun...unless you are effecting change)
8. I should <u>have</u>
9. I did not do <u>anything</u>! (Double negative: see *Fascinating Fact!* on the previous page.)
10. She <u>doesn't</u> like pizza.

VERB PHRASES

Here are three ways to identify a verb phrase:

A verb phrase might have two or more verbs
For example:

> We **will stay** at home.
> He **is studying** for an exam.
> She **will not go** there.
> You **might have said** something!

A verb phrase might be a verb with a preposition
For example: *give up, think over, turn down.*

A verb phrase might be a group of words with a verb and object but no subject
For example:

> **Hearing no reply,** she assumed he was out.
> **Rushing the test,** he finished too early.
> **To run a marathon,** I need to train hard.
> Close the door **to keep the noise out.**

Joke Break
If you're feeling sad, don't get in a lift. It might get you down.

WHY DO I NEED TO KNOW ABOUT VERB PHRASES?

1. Verb phrases add more meaning to a sentence. They provide more information about tenses and conditions. A summary of these is in the next chapter.

2. Verb phrases can be used to emphasise feelings, to quicken or to slow the pace of writing.

Example 1:* Song of Myself *by Walt Whitman

Walt Whitman was a nineteenth-century poet, essayist and journalist. Read this extract from his poem, entitled *Song of Myself:*

> *Have you reckon'd a thousand acres much? have you reckon'd the earth much?*
> *Have you practis'd so long to learn to read?*
> *Have you felt so proud to get at the meaning of poems?*
>
> *Stop this day and night with me and you shall possess the origin of all poems,*
> *You shall possess the good of the earth and sun, (there are millions of suns left,)*

Fascinating Fact!

The repetition of words at the beginning of a sentence or clause is called *anaphora.*

In the poem, Whitman employs anaphora with 'Have you', which he combines with verb phrases 'Have…reckon'd', 'Have…practis'd' and 'Have…felt' to create the impression that the poet is evaluating how much the reader has learnt. The pace is suitably slow, as he assesses the reader's readiness to develop further. In the next verse, the anaphora of 'You' combines with the verb phrase 'shall possess' to quicken the pace and change the mood. The poet now appears to be more positive and optimistic, promising fantastic things for the future.

Example 2:* Pride and Prejudice *by Jane Austen

After unsuccessfully trying to persuade her husband to visit Mr Bingley, who has just moved into the neighbourhood, Mrs Bennet declares in exasperation that she is sick of the sound of Mr Bingley's name. Mr Bennet, who has been pretending complete disinterest, then replies:

> *'If I **had known** as much this morning I certainly **would not have called on** him. It is very unlucky; but as I **have** actually **paid** the visit, we **cannot escape** the acquaintance now.'*

In this extract, the verb phrases slow the pace and create a sardonic mood. Mr Bennet clearly enjoys enunciating every syllable to observe and anticipate his wife's reaction.

Joke Break

PATIENT:	Doctor! Doctor! I can't sleep at night!
DOCTOR:	Lie on the edge of the bed. You'll soon drop off.

WHAT NEXT?

At GCSE, you don't need to learn the names of all the tenses in English, but it's interesting to see how the full range of verb phrases can convey different meanings. This also applies to the five types of conditional sentences. I would recommend casting your eyes over the next chapter and then beginning chapter 8, which introduces our next part of speech: pronouns.

Chapter 7: Verb Phrases in Tenses and the Conditionals

Verb phrases help you to form tenses. If you can understand tenses, you will be more aware of how to write accurately. You will also be better equipped in analytical essays to comment on the writer's choice of tense. The three main tenses are the past, the present and the future, which subdivide.

PAST TENSES

There are four past tenses, three of which always contain verb phrases. Let's begin by reviewing the simple past tense. It often doesn't contain verb phrases unless the verb has a preposition (for example, *to go up*).

The simple past tense

As we saw in the last chapter, we use the simple past tense to talk about finished past events or situations.

Example: First I <u>slept</u>. Then I <u>woke up</u>. After that, I <u>ate</u> my breakfast.

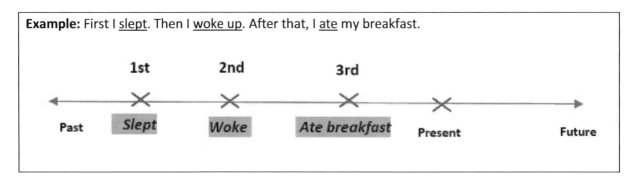

The past continuous tense (sometimes called the past progressive)

The verb phrase in the past continuous tense shows an unfinished action in the past.

Example: I <u>was running</u> in a marathon when I fainted with exhaustion.

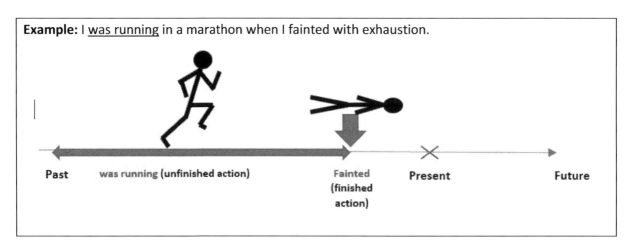

Fascinating Fact!

Did you know that verbs can also be nouns? For example:

Yesterday, I <u>was walking</u> (verb) to school when I saw a young child practising <u>a funny **walk**</u> (noun phrase).

The past perfect tense (sometimes called the pluperfect tense)

The verb phrase in the past perfect tense shows that something happened before another event in the past.

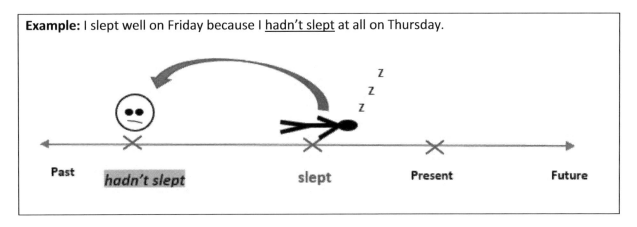

Example: I slept well on Friday because I <u>hadn't slept</u> at all on Thursday.

The past perfect continuous (or progressive) tense

The verb phrase in the past perfect continuous tense shows an unfinished action that was completed at some point in the past.

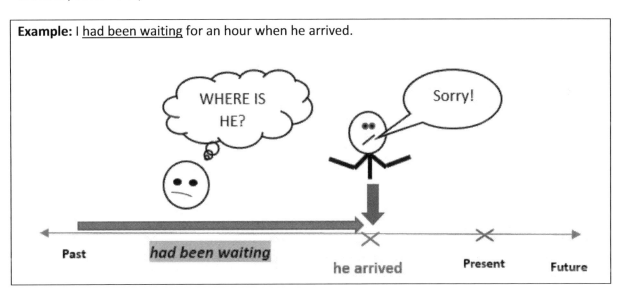

Example: I <u>had been waiting</u> for an hour when he arrived.

Common Mistakes with Verb Phrases in the Past Tense

Read the sentences below, underline the errors and then write the corrections.

Example: *On Tuesday, I was happy with the exam because I <u>revised</u> on Monday.* **had revised**

1. I thought I lost my keys, but then I found them.

2. I knew what was going to happen in the film because I read the book.

3. I never went to a football match before my friends dragged me to one last night.

Check your answers on the next page.

1. had lost
2. had read
3. had never been

All the corrections are in the past perfect tense. If you found this challenging, you're either American or influenced by American English. Although some Americans still use the past perfect tense, many use the simple past instead.

PRESENT TENSES

There are four present tense forms in English; let's begin with the simple present tense.

The simple present tense (sometimes called the present simple)
Like the simple past tense, most of the time there are no verb phrases unless the verb has a preposition. Often used with adverbs of frequency (e.g. *always, often, sometimes, seldom, never*), this tense describes something that you regularly do.

Example: I always <u>brush</u> my teeth twice a day.

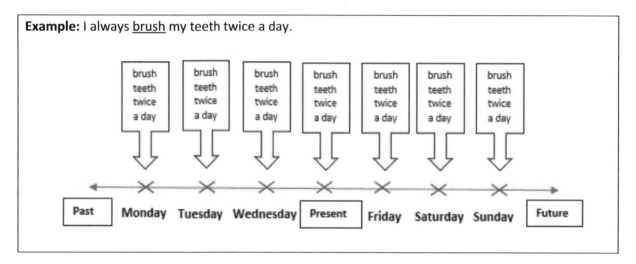

The present continuous tense (sometimes called the present progressive)
The verb phrase in the present continuous tense shows an unfinished action in the present time.

Example: Mum, this is a bad time to ring me! I <u>am running</u> a marathon!

The verb phrase in the present perfect tense is used in three different ways:

1. To talk about something that you have completed or not completed in your life.
It isn't important when this did or did not take place.

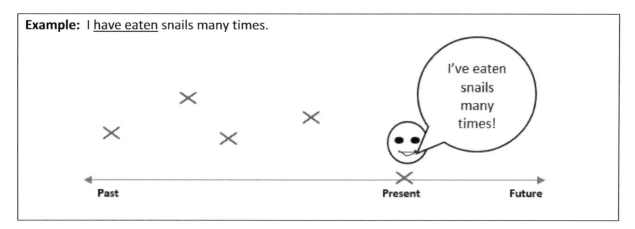

2. To talk about something that you have recently completed.

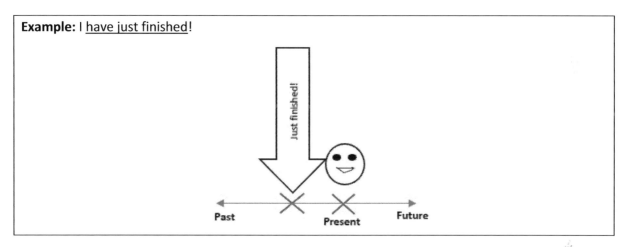

3. To talk about something that started in the past and is connected to the present. The focus is on the finished result.

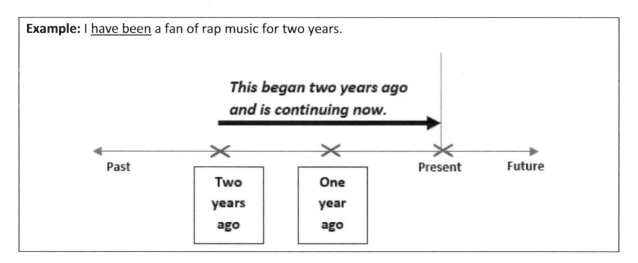

The present perfect continuous tense (sometimes called the present perfect progressive)

We use the verb phrase in this tense to describe something that started in the past and is connected to the present. The emphasis is on the length of time in which the event has been taking place:

I <u>have been yelling</u> for two hours!
(The focus is on the yelling.)
I <u>have been reading</u> the magazine that you lent me.
(The focus is on the reading.)

Example: I have been scrubbing this floor for two hours!

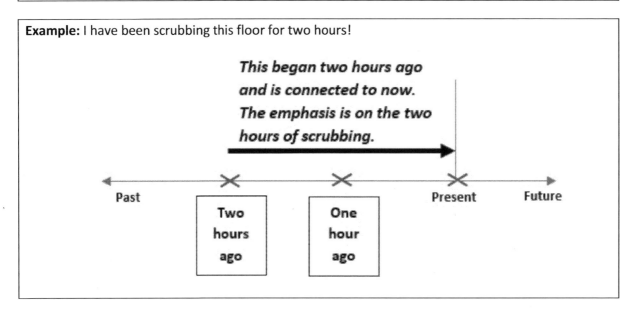

This began two hours ago and is connected to now. The emphasis is on the two hours of scrubbing.

Past — Two hours ago — One hour ago — Present — Future

Common Mistakes with Verb Phrases in the Present Tense

Read each sentence below, underline the error and then write the correction.

Example: *I never went* to Russia in my life. **have never been**

1. I did it already.

2. Did you finish yet?

3. I could of painted my bedroom pink.

1. I <u>have already done</u> it.
2. <u>Have you finished</u> yet?
3. I could <u>have</u> painted my bedroom pink.

If you think that questions 1 and 2 are correct, you might be influenced by American English. Many Americans use the simple past tense instead of the present perfect tense.

FUTURE TENSES

Some people argue that the future tense does not exist. Instead, verb phrases show ideas, plans and probability. Let's read some examples:

Will

To make a prediction, offer or promise about the future:

> It <u>will snow</u> tomorrow.
> My dad <u>will do</u> the washing up.
> I <u>will be</u> there in a minute!

Going to

For plans or intentions:

> When I get home, I <u>am going to tidy</u> my room.
> They <u>are going to move</u> to a new house.

Simple present tense

To talk about something arranged or scheduled:

> It <u>is</u> the end of term on Friday.
> The bus <u>leaves</u> in ten minutes.

Present continuous tense

For something arranged or planned:

> We <u>are catching</u> the 8.30 train.
> I <u>am having</u> a party on my birthday.

Modal verbs

1. The verbs *may, might* and *could* show that we're uncertain about the future:

> I <u>might not go out</u> tonight because I'm tired.
> We <u>could finish</u> now, but there's still a lot of work to do.

2. We can use *should* if we think something is likely to happen:

> We <u>should be</u> ready on time.
> The film <u>should finish</u> by ten o'clock.

The future continuous tense (or future progressive)

For emphasis when we are talking about intentions, arrangements or plans:

> I <u>will be thinking</u> of you!
> We won't get the bus; instead, we <u>will be walking</u> to school tomorrow.

To conclude this section, verb phrases can be used to convey a range of ideas to do with time. Imagine having to learn English as a second language!

THE CONDITIONALS

In the English language, there are five different ways to talk about things that might (not) happen, or might (not) have happened. These are called *conditional sentences*. In the examples below, it does not matter which clause comes first.

The zero conditional

We use this conditional to make statements that often relate to facts. The word *if* can be replaced with *when*, and the two clauses use the simple present tense:

> If (or when) you <u>freeze</u> water, it <u>turns</u> to ice.
> Water <u>turns</u> to ice if (or when) you <u>freeze</u> it.

The first conditional

This conditional makes statements about actions or events that are likely to happen in the future. The *if* clause uses the simple present tense and the other clause uses *will + infinitive:*

> If he <u>buys</u> the ingredients, they <u>will cook</u>.
> They <u>will cook</u> if he <u>buys</u> the ingredients.

The second conditional

This conditional describes an unlikely situation, and the structure is usually if + past simple and would + infinitive.

> If he <u>bought</u> the ingredients, they <u>would cook.</u>
> They <u>would cook</u> if he <u>bought</u> the ingredients.<u>_</u>
>
> If I <u>were</u>* rich, I <u>would buy</u> a castle.
> I <u>would buy</u> a castle If I <u>were</u>* rich.

*NB: With the second conditional, it's always I/you/he/she/it/we/they *were*.

The third conditional

This conditional describes something that did not happen in the past. The structure is usually if + past perfect and would + perfect infinitive:

> If he <u>had bought</u> the ingredients, they <u>would</u>* <u>have cooked</u>.
> They <u>would</u>* <u>have cooked</u> if he <u>had bought</u> the ingredients.

*You can also replace *would* with *could, might* or *may*.

Mixed conditionals

There are various ways to create mixed conditional sentences. The main thing to remember is that each clause refers to a different period of time:

> If I <u>had studied</u> harder for my exams, I <u>wouldn't be doing</u> this low-paid job. (past + present)
> If I <u>hadn't argued</u> with my friend, I<u>'d be going</u> on <u>holiday</u> with him to France. (past + future)

WHAT NEXT?

Well done! Before we review our next part of speech, let's finish with a well-deserved...

Joke Break

It's Christmas Eve. Ebenezer Scrooge wakes up to find a ghost at the foot of his bed.

    The ghost says, "I am the ghost of the third conditional. If you had behaved differently, I wouldn't have visited you."

Chapter 8: Pronouns

I hate scraping and cleaning my shoes. Dog walkers! If your dog does a poo, please put it in the bin!

...Put the *dog* in the bin? As the joke illustrates, we sometimes need to check that pronouns refer to the right noun.

WHAT'S A PRONOUN?

A pronoun replaces a noun, and there are different types of pronoun. For example:

Subject pronoun: *Julie and I played football.* → **We** *played football.*
Object pronoun: *Tom dropped his bag.* → *Tom dropped* **it**.
Possessive pronoun: *This is Shameel's coat.* → *This is* **his**.

For quick reference, here's a chart of pronouns that we use in English:

	SUBJECT PRONOUNS	**OBJECT PRONOUNS**	**DETERMINER** (Possessive Adjective)	**POSSESSIVE PRONOUNS**	**REFLEXIVE PRONOUNS**
1st person singular	I	me	my	mine	myself
2nd person singular	you	you	your	yours	yourself
3rd person singular	he/she/it	him/her/it	his/her/its	his/hers/--	himself/herself/itself
1st person plural	we	us	our	ours	ourselves
2nd person plural	you	you	your	yours	yourselves
3rd person plural	they	them	their	theirs	themselves

We're not going to examine all of these pronouns because, as a native speaker of English, you're likely to be using them correctly. Instead, this chapter will examine how you can use them in your writing. Then we'll look at some common mistakes.

HOW CAN MY KNOWLEDGE OF PRONOUNS IMPROVE MY WRITING?

Read the paragraph, below. What's wrong with it?

John went into town to do some shopping. John wandered around the Saturday market for a while and then John had some lunch. John went home. John wondered why his life seemed so boring. John felt that he was repeating himself all the time.

Yes, it's boring! Repeating John's name gets in the way and slows everything down. Pronouns therefore make your writing more fluent.

Pronoun suggestion

After mentioning a noun once, replace it with a pronoun for the rest of the paragraph:

> John went into town to do some shopping. He wandered around the Saturday market for a while and then he had some lunch. He went home. He wondered why his life seemed so boring. He felt that he was repeating himself all the time.

Better, yes, but this still sounds rather repetitive—we'll revise more interesting ways of starting sentences later in this guide.

Fascinating Fact: Political Correctness with Pronouns!

Another pronoun that is not yet archaic but has fallen into disuse is the third-person singular pronoun *one* to replace *he* or *she*. Nowadays, *one* sounds rather old-fashioned and formal. So what can we use instead? This is an interesting and at times a highly controversial subject:

- Some people replace the pronoun *one* with *he*. For example: *If a pupil does not understand, he should ask for help.*
- However, many females rightly feel that this pronoun excludes them. The solution? To add the pronoun *she*. For example: *If a pupil does not understand, he or she should ask for help.*
- This creates a stylistic challenge, as repeating *he or she* can become long-winded and clumsy after a while, especially in a long paragraph. Some people overcome this by replacing *he or she* with *s/he*. For example: *If a pupil does not understand, s/he should ask for help.*
- Others say that the forward slash jolts the sentence and makes it look ugly. A more popular solution is to use *they*. For example: *If a pupil does not understand, they should ask for help.* Grammatically, this is incorrect because the plural *they* refers to a singular *pupil*; nevertheless, this is becoming more widely accepted.
- There is also discussion about non-gendered pronouns. In Canada, for example, it is the law to use the pronouns of a non-gendered person's choice: *zir, ze* or *they*.

All of the above are fascinating examples of how language can change to reflect contemporary values. I wonder if, one day, an agreed solution will be to return to the third person singular *one*.

RELATIVE PRONOUNS

Common relative pronouns are *who, whose, which, that* and *what*. Always use *who* with people and *which/that/what* with things. We use them for different reasons:

To add extra information (non-defining clauses)
The relative pronouns *which* or *who* show that you're adding extra information: *I'm going to London, which isn't far.* The most important information is *I'm going to London*. The comma introduces the extra information, almost as an afterthought.

If the extra information is in the middle of a sentence, you need two commas, which act like brackets: *Erin, who's going to the party, scored full marks in the maths exam.* Erin scoring full marks in her maths exam is more important than the fact that she's going to the party (this is non-essential additional information which could delete if you wanted to).

Whose shows that something belongs to a person or animal. Again, we use a comma or commas to show that you're adding extra information: *Oli, whose stories gain top marks, has just published a book.*

To identify or define something or someone

Let's rework the above examples by removing the commas: *I'm going to London which isn't far.* With no comma, the meaning changes and the *which isn't far* is suddenly crucial to the sentence. If we were to place this in a context, we might say: *I know you want me to stay close to home because you worry about me. I won't be going far from home. I'm going to London which isn't far.*

Now let's rework the second example without commas: *Erin who's going to the party scored full marks in the maths exam.* Without the commas, the middle part of the sentence becomes vitally important. To put this in context, you might know two Erins, and so you ask your friend which Erin scored full marks in the maths exam. The answer would be *Erin who's going to the party scored full marks in the maths exam* (as opposed to Erin who is not going to the party).

The relative pronoun *whose* can refer to animals as well as people. Again, leave out the comma(s) when you identify someone or something: *That's the dog whose barking kept me awake all night.* Although it's less common, *whose* can also be used to show possession with a thing: *The book whose pages are torn needs to be repaired.*

There's also no comma before *that* or *what* when they define things:

Person A: Which shoes shall I wear?
Person B: Does it matter <u>what</u> I think? Wear the shoes <u>that</u> you wore to your sister's wedding.

The pronoun *what* identifies the thoughts of the speaker. The pronoun *that* identifies one particular pair of shoes: no others will do.

Yourself!

Choose a pronoun from the list and put it in the spaces below: *who, whom, whose, which, that, what, yourself, themselves.* Check your answers on the next page.

1. You should hear _____ talk!

2. I like music _____ makes me want to dance.

3. _____ book is this?

4. Lots of students, _____ could get excellent exam results, are in this school.

5. I don't understand _____ is happening.

6. I love bread _____ my gran has baked.

7. They're introducing _____ to everyone.

8. People _____ live in glass houses shouldn't throw stones.

9. _____ are you going to invite?

10. That's Karim, _____ happens to be in my class.

11. A GCSE revision guide, _____ was written by Mr Bruff, is a number one best seller on Amazon.

12. That's the girl _____ singing's so good _____ she's joining a group.

Before you check your answers, consider how the commas affect meaning.

1. You should hear <u>yourself</u> talk!
2. I like music <u>which/that</u> makes me want to dance. (There's no comma because it's identifying which music makes me want to dance.)
3. <u>Whose</u> book is this?
4. Lots of students, <u>who</u> could get excellent exam results, are in this school. (Remember that *who* is always used with people: never *that*. The commas are like brackets and so the focus is on lots of people at the school.)
5. I don't understand <u>what</u> is happening. (There's no comma because *what* identifies what is not understood.)
6. I love bread <u>which/that</u> my gran has baked. (There's no comma because <u>which/that</u> identify gran's bread.)
7. They're introducing <u>themselves</u> to everyone.
8. People <u>who</u> live in glass houses shouldn't throw stones. (There's no comma because *who* is identifying which particular people should not throw stones.)
9. <u>Whom</u> are you going to invite? (Yes, *who* is more common, but grammatically, *whom* is the correct answer because it's an object pronoun.)
10. That's Karim, <u>who</u> happens to be in my class. (There's a comma because *who* introduces extra information.)
11. A GCSE revision guide, <u>which</u> was written by Mr Bruff, is a number one best seller on Amazon. (The commas act like brackets because *which* introduces extra information. You can only have *that* if you remove the commas and you're defining which particular revision guide is number 1 i.e. the one written by Mr Bruff.)
12. That's the girl <u>whose</u> singing's so good <u>that</u> she's joining a group. (No commas because you are identifying which girl's singing is so good.)

Joke Break
Teacher: Give me two pronouns!
Pupil: Who? Me?

REFLEXIVE PRONOUNS

Reflexive Pronouns

Reflexive pronouns are used to talk about things that you do to yourself. Example: *Emma pinched herself*. How well do you know the others?

Test Yourself!

Fill each gap with a reflexive pronoun and check your answers at the bottom of the page.

1. My dad cut _____ with a sharp knife.

2. After a shower, I dried _____ with a towel.

3. They enjoyed _____ at the beach.

4. Watch out! Oh, no! Did you hurt _____?

5. She took a deep breath and prepared _____ to meet her boyfriend's parents.

6. Shall we buy that textbook and teach _____ Spanish?

7. Children! Behave _____!

1. himself
2. myself
3. themselves
4. yourself
5. herself
6. ourselves
7. yourselves

Fascinating Fact!

The pronouns *thou, thee, thy, thine* and *thyself* are archaic second-person pronouns, no longer used in everyday speech. In Shakespeare's time, people used *thou* when talking to social inferiors or to show intimacy between lovers, a husband and wife or close friends. The pronoun *you* was a formal word in a similar way to *vous* in French and *usted* in Spanish. By the 17th century, people had replaced *thou* with *you*. Nowadays, *thou* is used in formal religious contexts, as regional dialect in pockets of Northern England, and in Scots.

Joke Break

Two English teachers, whose favourite part of speech is a pronoun, get married. Standing at the aisle, they exchange their wedding vows.
     The vicar says, "I now pronouns you he and she."

Common Mistakes with Pronouns

There's one pronoun mistake in every sentence below. Underline the pronoun error, write the correction and explain your correction. Check your answers on the next page.

1. Me and my friend wrote a song.
   Correct answer and explanation:

2. My brother and me play in a band.
   Correct answer and explanation:

3. The delivery man gave my mum, my dad and I a huge parcel.
   Correct answer and explanation:

4. Molly, who's mother is a doctor, loves animals.
   Correct answer and explanation:

5. There's the man that stole your phone!
   Correct answer and explanation:

Answers and Explanations

1. <u>Me and my friend</u> wrote a song. Correct answer: *My friend and I.* Reason: (1) If you delete *my friend* you would be left with *Me wrote a song.* This doesn't make sense. You would say *I wrote a song.* (2) It's good manners to mention yourself last.
2. <u>My brother and me</u> play in a band. Correct answer: *My brother and I.* Reason: (1) Similarly, if you delete *My brother* you would be left with *Me play in a band*, which doesn't make sense. You would say *I play in a band.* (2) Again, show off your manners!
3. The delivery man gave <u>my mum, my dad and I</u> a huge parcel. Correct answer: *my mum, my dad and me.* Reason: If you were to delete *my mum* and *my dad*, you would be left with *The delivery man gave I a huge parcel*, which doesn't make sense. You would say *The delivery man gave <u>me</u> a huge parcel.*
4. Molly, <u>who's</u> mother is a doctor, loves animals. Correct answer: *whose.* Reason: *whose* shows that this is the mother of Molly. The word *who's* is short for *who is.*
5. There's the man <u>that</u> stole your phone! Correct answer: *who.* Reason: *that* is for things, not people. The man is a living, breathing human being, so *who* is the correct answer.

An adjective describes a noun. Did you know that when you use a list of adjectives, they're always in a particular order? For example: *I'd love a beautiful, spacious, rectangular, new, green, British, grass lawn.* The word order is:

Determiner:	a, the, etc.
What you notice:	beautiful, ugly, interesting, boring, etc.
Size:	spacious, big, small, etc.
Shape:	rectangular, triangular, square, round, etc.
Age:	new, old, etc.
Colour:	green, blue, yellow, etc.
Origin:	British, French, etc.
Material:	grass, wooden, gold, silver, etc.

There are great advantages of speaking English as a first language. One of them is that you follow grammar rules without even realising it!

Test Yourself!

Charles Dickens is famous for his use of vivid adjectives. In this extract from *Great Expectations*, the narrator Pip describes an early memory of visiting the graves of his parents and brothers. Then an escaped convict appears. Find and underline the twenty-five adjectives in this extract.

Vocabulary Key
Bleak: depressing
Marshes: low wet land with different types of grass growing on it
Leaden: the dull grey colour of lead
Lair: (1) where a wild animal lives or (2) a criminal's secret hiding place
Iron: Shackles, made of iron (two metal fastenings, one for each leg, with a connecting chain to stop a prisoner running).

My first most vivid and broad impression of the identity of things seems to me to have been gained on a memorable raw afternoon towards evening. At such a time I found out for certain that this bleak place overgrown with nettles was the churchyard; [...] and that the dark flat wilderness beyond the churchyard, [...] with scattered cattle feeding on it, was the marshes; and that the low leaden line beyond was the river; and that the distant savage lair from which the wind was rushing was the sea; and that the small bundle of shivers growing afraid of it all and beginning to cry, was Pip.

"Hold your noise!" cried a terrible voice, as a man started up from among the graves at the side of the church porch. "Keep still, you little devil, or I'll cut your throat!"

A fearful man, all in coarse gray, with a great iron on his leg. A man with no hat, and with broken shoes...

You might have noticed how the adjectives create a sad mood, which changes to hints of danger and then fear. This fear is developed through noun phrases in the final paragraph, creating a sense of being overwhelmed.

My _first_ most _vivid_ and _broad_ impression of the identity of things seems to me to have been gained on a _memorable_ _raw_ afternoon towards evening. At such a time I found out for _certain_ that this _bleak_ place _overgrown_ with nettles was the churchyard; [...] and that the _dark_ _flat_ wilderness beyond the churchyard, [...] with _scattered_ cattle feeding on it, was the marshes; and that the _low_ _leaden_ line beyond was the river; and that the _distant_ _savage_ lair from which the wind was rushing was the sea; and that the _small_ bundle of shivers growing _afraid_ of it all and beginning to cry, was Pip.

"Hold your noise!" cried a _terrible_ voice, as a man started up from among the graves at the side of the church porch. "Keep _still_, you _little_ devil, or I'll cut your throat!"

A _fearful_ man, all in _coarse_ _gray_*, with a _great_ iron on his leg. A man with no hat, and with _broken_ shoes...

*It's understood that these adjectives describe clothes (noun). Note the different spelling of 'grey', which is still used in America today.

COMMAS IN LISTS OF ADJECTIVES

We use commas to separate a list of adjectives—remember that there's no comma between the final adjective and noun. For example: _She crossed the dangerous, swinging, creaking bridge._

Sometimes, adjectives describe the same part of a noun. If this happens, don't use a comma. For example: _He has dark brown eyes. Dark_ and _brown_ both describe the <u>colour</u> of his eyes, so there's no comma.

Insert the commas if they are needed. Check your answers on the next page.

1. I bought some apples, bananas, oranges and grapes.

2. The little old lady crossed the road.

3. She has a lot of green cotton t-shirts.

4. He is a tall, dark handsome man.

5. She's wearing a pale yellow tracksuit.

6. He gave his girlfriend an antique gold ring.

7. Her short, blonde greasy hair needs a good wash.

8. The hotel is large, comfortable and affordable.

9. I gazed in wonder at the vast open sea.

10. Congratulations! You have a strong, healthy baby girl!

Fascinating Fact!

You can make noun phrases with adjectives. For example:
the <u>purring, fluffy, flea-bitten</u> cat

---

1. I bought some apples, bananas, oranges and grapes.
2. The little old lady crossed the road.
3. She has a lot of green cotton t-shirts.
4. He is a tall, dark, handsome man.
5. She's wearing a pale yellow tracksuit.
6. He gave his girlfriend an antique gold ring.
7. Her short, blonde, greasy hair needs a good wash.
8. The hotel is large, comfortable and affordable.
9. I gazed in wonder at the vast open sea.
10. Congratulations! You have a strong, healthy baby girl!

Fascinating Fact!

Many people say that you should use a comma where you would naturally pause when speaking. This comes from a time when texts were either recited from memory or were read out loud. Punctuation helped to break texts down into shorter, more understandable chunks. Early Christians started to develop the idea of punctuation as a way of helping priests to read aloud from the Bible. When the printing press was invented in the fifteenth century, punctuation marks became more standardised, and some even disappeared. Today, silent reading is more common than reading out loud, and punctuation rules are more firmly in place. The comma is the most used—or perhaps the most misused—punctuation mark of them all.

COMPOUND ADJECTIVES

Do you remember compound nouns, two or more nouns that make one noun? In chapter 3, we read the examples *football* and *sister-in-law*. There are also compound adjectives, and these are always joined with a hyphen. For example: *Let's look at the <u>long-term</u> weather forecast.*

It's also common to see them with a number. For example: *I live in a <u>three-bedroom</u> house where my <u>eleven-year-old</u> brother has celebrated his birthday.*

Fascinating Fact!

Compound adjectives can make sentences easier to understand. What is the difference in meaning between these sentences?

> *Look! A man-eating snake!*
> *Look! A man eating snake!*

> *I teach eight-year-old children.*
> *I teach eight year-old children.*

Check your answers on the next page.

Joke Break
A student brags, "I'm so adjective, I verb nouns!"

WHY DO I NEED TO KNOW ABOUT ADJECTIVES?

Adjectives make your sentences more interesting. But be careful! What's the effect of placing adjectives in front of every noun? Read the example:

It was a warm spring day. A happy, tall, pretty, eleven-year-old child skipped towards the huge, welcoming woodland park. The ancient creaking trees swayed in the fresh, flower-scented breeze. The delighted girl tossed her bright red plastic coat onto an empty, dry, wooden bench.

It becomes too much after a while, doesn't it? This is called overwriting: don't put an adjective in front of every noun!

Common Mistakes

Find and underline the four errors in the following paragraph. Then check your answers overleaf.

How am I? I'm good, thanks. I had a fun time at the party last Saturday. In fact, it was the funnest party I've ever been to. It was so fun!

ADJECTIVE (OR ADJECTIVAL) PHRASES

An adjective phrase is a group of words that provides more detail about a noun or pronoun:

> And each <u>separate dying</u> ember wrought its ghost upon the floor.
> —*The Raven*, Edgar Allan Poe
> It was <u>cold, bleak, biting</u> weather.
> —*A Christmas Carol*, Charles Dickens

As well as coming before a noun or pronoun, an adjective phrase can be after the noun or pronoun (noun phrase). For example: *incredibly boring* game. It is *incredibly boring*.

Sometimes a verb might link an adjective phrase to a noun phrase. For example:

> *The tapestry* (noun phrase) *is* (verb) *beautifully woven by my cousins* (adjective phrase).
> *Your skirt* *looks* (verb) *far too short* (adjective phrase).

Fascinating Fact!

An adjective phrase can sit inside a noun phrase. For example: *That beautifully woven tapestry is worth a lot of money.* The adjective phrase *beautifully woven* sits inside the noun phrase *That beautifully woven tapestry.*

Adjective phrases make your sentences more interesting. The beginning of this sentence is quite boring: *The exciting and action-packed film delighted the audience.*

Now put the adjective phrase at the beginning of the sentence and separate it with a comma: *Exciting and action-packed, the film delighted the audience.*

Congratulations! Your English teacher or examiner has proof that you can vary your sentences.

Answers to Common Mistakes Questions

How am I? I'm good, (1) thanks. I had a fun (2) time at the party last Saturday. In fact, it was the funnest (3) party I've ever been to. It was so (4) fun!

(1) *Good* is an adjective—are you saying that you're well behaved or that you're good at something? Use the adverb *well* instead. Alternative answers, depending on your level of formality: *very well, fine.*
(2) You can't use *fun* in front of a noun because *fun* is a noun. The only time you can use *fun* to describe something is when it follows a verb to describe a subject. For example: *It was fun*. The word *fun* is overused and boring, anyway. Show off your vocabulary!
(3) This is wrong—see point (2).
(4) Either say: *It was so much fun!* OR *It was such fun!*

Joke Break
I think it's incredibly weird when a sentence doesn't end the way you think it onomatopoeia.

Common Mistakes

Which of these sentences is correct?

She is my bestest friend.
Raj is more quick than Mark.
Which is best—milk or juice?

Answer

None of them! Let's look at why:

COMPARATIVE AND SUPERLATIVE ADJECTIVES

Adjectives are used for comparing. If you compare two people or things, you're making a comparative sentence. For example: *Milk is better than juice.*

When you compare three or more people or things, you are making a superlative sentence. For example: *She is my best friend.* (You have at least three friends.)

Because you're a native speaker of English, most of the time you use the correct grammar when you compare. However, there might be the occasional error, so...

How good is your knowledge of comparative and superlative adjectives? Fill in the gaps with the correct form of the adjective in brackets. For example: *I'm <u>older than</u> (old) my brother. However, he cooks the <u>most delicious</u> (delicious) pasta in the world!*

1. I'm_____ (tall) my father.

2. Daffodils are _____(popular) than roses.

3. The _____(expensive) thing I own is my car.

4. My teacher is _____(wise) person I know.

5. My friend is much _____(happy) than she used to be.

6. This is the_____(wet) day of the year so far.

7. Which is _____(good)—milk or juice?

8. Who's the_____(famous) person in the world?

9. She has _____(many) clothes than me.

10. That poor boy has the_____(bad) exam results in the year group.

Answers

1. I'm <u>taller than</u> my father.
2. Daffodils are <u>more popular</u> than roses.
3. The <u>most expensive</u> thing I own is my car.
4. My teacher is <u>the wisest</u> person I know.
5. My friend is much <u>happier</u> than she used to be.
6. This is the <u>wettest</u> day of the year so far.
7. Which is <u>better</u>—milk or juice?
8. Who's the <u>most famous</u> person in the world?
9. She has <u>more</u> clothes than me.
10. That poor boy has the <u>worst</u> exam results in the year group.

If any of your answers are wrong or misspelt, study the reference charts on the next page. They contain the spelling rules as well as a summary of how to form comparative and superlative adjectives.

Joke Break
Comparative Joke:
Question: What gets wetter the more it dries?
Answer: A towel.
Superlative Joke:
Question: What's the longest word in the English language?
Answer: *Smiles* because there's a mile between the first and last letter.

HOW TO FORM COMPARATIVE AND SUPERLATIVE ADJECTIVES

Rules	Comparative	Superlative
Words of one syllable		
add –er or *–est* quick	quicker	quickest
If word ends in *–e*, add *–r* or *-st* wise	wiser	wisest
If word ends in consonant & vowel & consonant, double the final consonant. Then add *–er* or *–est* big	bigger	biggest
Words of two syllables		
If word ends in *–le* or *–ow,* add *–r/-er* or *-st/-est* gentle yellow	gentler yellower	gentlest yellowest
If the word ends in *-y*, change to *–ier* or *-iest* happy	happier	happiest
All other words, add *more* or *most* tranquil	more tranquil	most tranquil
Words of three syllables or more **Add *more* or *most*** beautiful	more beautiful	most beautiful

IRREGULAR COMPARATIVE AND SUPERLATIVE ADJECTIVES

Adjective	Comparative	Superlative
good	better	best
bad	worse	worst
far	farther/further	farthest/furthest
little	less	least
many	more	most
much	more	most

Joke Break
Did you know that the starfish is the most famous fish in the ocean?

Chapter 10: Prepositions

Person A: Can I tell you a joke?
Person B: Sure!
Person A: At, on, under, above, next to, around, during, after, beside.
Person B: That's awful! Are you trying to preposition me?

WHAT'S A PREPOSITION?

There are two categories of preposition:

Prepositions of Place	Prepositions of Time
Definition: Tells you where something is.	**Definition:** Provides information about time.
Example: *The cat sat <u>on</u> the mat.*	**Example:** *I'll see you <u>before</u> three o'clock.*
Other examples: *above across against along around behind beside between by down in in front of into near next next to of over through under up*	**Other examples:** *after at before during in on*

Test Yourself!

Prepositions of Place

Read the sentences and fill in the gaps. Then check your answers on the next page.

1.   The boy hid_____ the bush.

2.   My pen is _____the floor.

3.   The car is parked _____ the garage.

4.   The couple walked _____the garden.

5.   A lorry rumbled _____ the road.

Prepositions of Time

Read the sentences and fill in the gaps. Then check your answers on the next page.

1.   _____ the Middle Ages, most people only washed their hands and faces.

2.   All of Year 7 were born _____ this century.

3.   I'm going to the gym _____ Saturday.

4.   Tomorrow, let's go out _____ 10 o'clock.

5.   _____ 10pm _____ Sunday, I fell asleep.

Fascinating Fact!
You can make noun phrases with prepositions:
cat on the fence
cat in the garden

Sometimes, more than one answer is possible. The most likely ones are below.

Prepositions of Place

1. The boy hid behind/in/under/next to the bush.
2. My pen is on the floor.
3. The car is parked in the garage.
4. The couple walked into/in/around the garden.
5. A lorry rumbled down/along/up the road.

Prepositions of Time

1. During/In the Middle Ages, most people only washed their hands and faces.
2. All of Year 7 were born in this century.
3. I'm going to the gym on Saturday.
4. Tomorrow, let's go out at/before/after 10 o'clock.
5. At/Before/After 10pm on Sunday, I fell asleep.

AMERICAN AND BRITISH PREPOSITIONS

Did you know that we've been influenced by the American culture so much that some people use American prepositions without knowing it? How good is your knowledge of British English? Fill in the gaps, below. Warning! Two British English phrases don't need a preposition, so leave those spaces blank.

American English	British English
1. Monday through Friday	1. Monday _____ Friday
2. On the weekend	2. _____ the weekend
3. To talk with someone.	3. To talk _____ someone.
4. To meet with someone	4. To meet _____ someone
5. Different from/than	5. Different from/_____
6. To get off of a bus.	6. To get off _____ a bus.
7. A quarter after three	7. A quarter _____ three
8. In school	8. _____ school
9. Fill out a form	9. Fill _____ a form
10. Mad at someone	10. Angry _____ someone

Now check your answers on the next page.

Joke Break	
Person A:	OK, I give in.
Person B:	You can't end a sentence with a preposition!
Person A:	OK, I in give.

61

American English	British English
1. Monday through Friday	1. Monday <u>to</u> Friday
2. On the weekend	2. <u>At</u> the weekend
3. To talk with someone.	3. To talk <u>to</u> someone.
4. To meet with someone	4. To meet someone
5. Different from/than	5. Different from/<u>to</u>
6. To get off of a bus.	6. To get off a bus.
7. A quarter after three	7. A quarter <u>past</u> three
8. In school	8. <u>At</u> school
9. Fill out a form	9. Fill <u>in</u> a form
10. Mad at someone	10. Angry <u>with</u> someone

Fascinating Fact!

The joke on the previous page references an old grammar rule about not ending a sentence with a preposition. This rule, like the rule about the split infinitive, is based on Latin. By way of example, it would be wrong to say: *He tried his new jeans <u>on</u>.* Instead, it should be: *He tried <u>on</u> his new jeans.*

Many people object to this rule because it doesn't sit well with English grammar. We have two types of verbs that end with prepositions:
- Phrasal verbs, which can be split. E.g. *<u>To add</u> some numbers <u>up</u>, to break a problem <u>down</u>.*
- Prepositional verbs, which can't be split. E.g. *<u>to run out of</u> milk, <u>to apply for</u> a job.*

If you try to rephrase prepositional verbs, it can sound rather silly, as we saw with the joke. Here's another example: *This is the kind of bad behaviour up with which I will not put.*

PREPOSITIONAL PHRASES

A prepositional phrase contains a preposition and a noun or a pronoun. It answers the questions *When?* or *Where?* For example:

Where? *At the museum*
When? *In the afternoon*

Fascinating Fact!

The English language is constantly evolving. When people create new verbs with prepositions, we intuitively understand what they mean. For example, celebrity cook Delia Smith said that she was 'reciped out' when she announced in 2003 that she was going to retire from making cookery programmes for television.

WHAT'S THE DIFFERENCE BETWEEN A NOUN PHRASE AND A PREPOSITIONAL PHRASE?

1. With a prepositional phrase, the noun or pronoun are the **object** of the preposition. Example:

> **Where?**
> *on the fence*
>
> **Explanation:** The *fence* is the **object** of this phrase, so it's a prepositional phrase.

2. A noun phrase can have a prepositional phrase, but it modifies the **subject** of the sentence:

> *the cat on the fence*
>
> **Explanation:** The cat is the **subject** of the phrase. The prepositional phrase adds more information about the cat, so this group of words is a noun phrase.

WHY DO I NEED TO KNOW ABOUT PREPOSITIONAL PHRASES?

1. You can use them to make your sentences more interesting
Study the example sentences:

Where?		When?	
A:	The dragon slept in a dark cave.	A:	I wake up early at the weekend.
B:	In a dark cave, the dragon slept.	B:	At the weekend, I wake up early.

With both examples, B is more impressive. Why? It's evidence that you can vary your sentences. **REMEMBER:** When you begin a sentence with a prepositional phrase, always use a comma!

2. You can craft your sentences to convey ideas
Read the extracts, below:

> <u>For a long time</u>, I went to bed early.
> —*Swann's Way,* Marcel Proust
>
> *As proud parents sat open-mouthed <u>on the surrounding benches</u>, she came hurtling <u>out of the back annex</u>, <u>along the corridor</u>, <u>through the connecting door</u>, <u>into the hall</u>, <u>up to the springboard</u> and <u>into space</u>.*
> —*Unreliable Memoirs,* Clive James

The prepositional phrase in the first extract is in the opening sentence of Proust's novel. It answers the question **When?** Proust deliberately uses the prepositional phrase to hook the reader, who wants to know the significance of this time in the past and the events surrounding it. It is also implies that he does not go to bed early now, which poses more questions.

In the second extract, the underlined prepositional phrases answer the question **Where?** They build momentum, creating the impression of a whirlwind of energy and movement.

WHAT NEXT?

"I wish I had a pet tiger!" said the child wildly.
Can you guess the next part of speech that we're going to revise?

Chapter 11: Adverbs

"I wish I had a pet tiger!" said the child wildly.
"I have stomach ache!" said the triangle acutely.
"I'll email you again," said the employee resentfully.

These adverbial jokes are called Tom Swifties after a character in a series of adventure novels by Edward L. Stratemeyer. Each adverb links to what's being said and contains a pun (a play on words).

WHAT'S AN ADVERB?

An adverb describes a verb, and most adverbs end in –ly. For example: *They are singing beautifully.*

Although many adverbs follow a verb, some are before a verb to add emphasis. For example: *I totally agree with you!*

WHY DO I NEED TO KNOW ABOUT ADVERBS?

Study these examples:

The job applicant <u>nervously</u> answered the questions.
<u>Nervously,</u> the job applicant answered the questions.

The second sentence is a more interesting one for your teacher or examiner. Begin a sentence with an adverb, put a comma after it and—congratulations! We have evidence that you can vary your sentences.

THE SPELLING OF ADVERBS

1. In most cases, add -ly to an adjective to make an adverb
Example: *bright → brightly*

2. When the word has two syllables and ends in –y, change the -y to –i
Example: *happy → happily*

3. When the word ends with a consonant plus –le, drop the -e and only add –y
Example: *comfortable → comfortably.* (The –*l* is already there, so there is no need to add another one.)

Commonly Misspelt Adverbs

All of the adverbs below are spelt wrongly. Correct the spelling and then check your answers on the next page.

1. completly →

2. definately →

3. realy →

4. unfortunatly →

5. incidently →

6. immediaty →

1. **Completely:** add –*ly*. There is no need to drop the final –*e* with *complete* (see rule 3 on previous page for when to do this).
2. **Definitely:** This is an ordinary spelling mistake. Spelling tip: *I can defi<u>nite</u>ly see a <u>nit</u>!*
3. **Really:** add –*ly*. It doesn't make any difference that the word *real* already ends in –*l*.
4. **Unfortunately:** add –*ly*. You don't drop the final –*e* with *unfortunate* (see rule 3 on previous page for when to do this).
5. **Incidentally:** add –*ly*. It doesn't make any difference that the word *incidental* ends in –*l*.
6. **Immediately:** add –*ly*. You don't drop the final –*e* with *immediate* (see rule 3 on previous page for when to do this).

Test Yourself! Adverbs in Literature

Read this extract from *The Withered Arm* by Thomas Hardy in which the sleeping Rhoda has a nightmare about her ex-boyfriend's new wife. How many adverbs can you find? Underline them and check your answers on the next page.

...the blue eyes peered cruelly into her face: and then the figure thrust forward its left hand mockingly, so as to make the wedding-ring it wore glitter in Rhoda's eyes. Maddened mentally, and nearly suffocated by pressure, the sleeper struggled...

ADVERBS AND ADJECTIVES

Some people confuse adverbs with adjectives because some adjectives also end in –*ly*. For example: *He is a <u>lonely</u> man.* In this sentence, *lonely* describes the noun *man*, so *lonely* is an adjective. Remember:

- An ad**verb** describes a **verb**.
- An adjective describes a noun.

Test Yourself! Adverb and Adjective Identification Exercise

Are the underlined words adverbs or adjectives? Write your answer after each sentence and then check your answers on the next page.

1. Sarah munches the sandwich <u>slowly.</u>

2. Our team won although we are <u>unlikely</u> heroes.

3. Jay sings <u>beautifully.</u>

4. Athletes can run <u>quickly</u>.

5. That's an <u>ugly</u> gargoyle.

> **Joke Break**
> "You must recycle tins!" she said candidly.
> I'll keep my thoughts to myself," said the fish deeply.

> *...the blue eyes peered <u>cruelly</u> into her face: and then the figure thrust forward its left hand <u>mockingly</u>, so as to make the wedding-ring it wore glitter in Rhoda's eyes. Maddened <u>mentally</u>, and <u>nearly</u> suffocated by pressure, the sleeper struggled...*

You might have underlined some adverbs that don't end in –*ly*. If so, well done! We'll revise those in a minute.

Answers to Adverb and Adjective Identification Exercise

1. Sarah munches the sandwich <u>slowly.</u> **adverb**
2. Our team won although we are <u>unlikely</u> heroes. **adjective**
3. Jay sings <u>beautifully.</u> **adverb**
4. Athletes can run <u>quickly.</u> **adverb**
5. That's an <u>ugly</u> gargoyle. **adjective**

Other Adverbs

Some adverbs don't end in –*ly* because they have other purposes:

- **PLACE:** They tell us <u>where</u> the verb is happening. Example: *He is singing <u>there</u>.* Many adverbs of manner also show movement in a particular direction, ending in -*ward* or -*wards*.
- **TIME:** They tell us <u>when</u> the verb is happening. Example: *She is singing <u>tomorrow.</u>*
- **MANNER:** They tell us <u>how</u> the verb is happening. Example: *He is walking <u>barefoot.</u>*
- **FREQUENCY:** They tell us how <u>frequently</u> the verb is happening. Example: *She <u>often</u> goes home.*

Test Yourself!

Let's revisit part of *The Withered Arm* extract. Can you find an adverb to do with TIME and another to do with PLACE? Check your answers on the next page.

> *...the blue eyes peered cruelly into her face: and then the figure thrust forward its left hand...*

Common Mistakes with Adverbs

Below is a mixture of right and wrong sentences. Tick the correct sentences and write the correction next to each wrong sentence. Check your answers on the next page.

1. He didn't steal anything! He's a <u>good</u> boy!

2. How are you? I'm <u>good.</u>

3. She did really <u>well</u> in the exam.

4. She did <u>good.</u>

5. He did it <u>quick</u>.

Joke Break
"This is the best iron I've ever used!" said the man impressively.

> *...the blue eyes peered cruelly into her face: and **then** [TIME] the figure thrust **forward** [PLACE] its left hand...*

Answers and Explanations

1. Correct: the adjective *good* describes the noun *boy*.
2. Wrong because the speaker is using an adjective instead of an adverb (see adjectives chapter). The correct answer, depending on your level of formality, should be: *Fine, thanks. / Well, thanks / I'm very well, thank you.*
3. Correct: *well* is an adverb which describes the verb *did*.
4. Wrong because this should be *she did well*. The speaker is using an adjective instead of an adverb.
5. Wrong because an adjective has been used instead of an adverb. This should be *He did it quickly*.

COMPARATIVE AND SUPERLATIVE ADVERBS

Hold on a moment! I hear you cry. *Haven't we already done this?* Yes, with adjectives. You can also use adverbs to make comparative and superlative sentences. With adjectives, you add *–er* and *–est* to form comparatives and superlatives. To form a comparative or superlative adverb, you can sometimes do this. You can also add *more/most*. Examples:

> He arrived <u>sooner</u> than me.
> We worked <u>the hardest</u> to finish early.
>
> She plays touch rugby <u>more confidently</u> after a term of practice.
> Our old-fashioned landline is used the <u>least frequently</u> in the house.

Test Yourself!

Use the adverbs in brackets to make comparative and superlative sentences. Remember that not all adverbs end in *-ly!* When you have finished, check your answers on the next page.

1. He always works _____ (hard) than me.

2. What was my time? Did I run the _____ (fast)?

3. You need to write more _____ (carefully)!

4. In the spelling test, I did the _____ (bad) in the class.

5. I can run _____ (far) than you.

6. She dances the most_____ (crazily) of all the people at the nightclub.

7. He gets out of bed _____ (early) than her.

8. My cousin draws _____ (well).

9. She speaks Italian more _____ (beautifully) than me.

10. He speaks the most_____ (thoughtfully) in the class.

1. He always works <u>harder</u> (hard) than me.
2. What was my time? Did I run the <u>fastest</u> (fast)?
3. You need to write <u>more carefully</u> (carefully)!
4. In the spelling test, I did the <u>worst</u> (bad) in the class.
5. I can run <u>farther</u> (far) than you.
6. She dances the <u>most crazily</u> (crazily) of all the people at the nightclub.
7. He gets out of bed <u>earlier</u> (early) than her.
8. My cousin draws <u>better</u> or <u>best</u> (well).
9. She speaks Italian <u>more beautifully</u> (beautifully) than me.
10. He speaks the <u>most thoughtfully</u> (thoughtfully) in the class.

HOW TO FORM COMPARATIVE AND SUPERLATIVE ADVERBS

Rules	Comparative	Superlative
Adverbs of one syllable: Add *–er* or *–est* fast	fast<u>er</u>	fast<u>est</u>
Adverbs of more than one syllable, ending in –ly: Add *more/most or less/least* happily thoughtfully	<u>more</u> happily <u>less</u> happily <u>more</u> thoughtfully <u>less</u> thoughtfully	<u>most</u> happily <u>least</u> happily <u>most</u> thoughtfully <u>least</u> thoughtfully
Adverbs that are the same as an adjective both have more than one syllable: Add *–er* or *–est* early*	earlier	earliest

NB: y →i

IRREGULAR COMPARATIVES AND SUPERLATIVES

Adverb	Comparative	Superlative
badly	worse	worst
well	better	best
far	farther	farthest
little	less	least

Joke Break

"I'll have a dozen cupcakes!" said the girl abundantly.

"Would you like your fortune told?" asked the lady charmingly.

"The escaped convict is camping," said the boy contentedly.

All the adverb jokes in this chapter are based on puns, which play on the sound of words to achieve a particular effect. The first-century Roman orators (speech writers and speakers) Cicero and Quintilianus believed that the ability to make puns was a sign of intellectual suppleness. But which are the oldest recorded puns in English?

The Bible is one of the earliest books to be translated into English, and it contained many puns. Although they apparently sound great in Hebrew and Aramaic, not all of them have translated well into English. However, some have. Saint Peter was the first pope, and the name Peter means *rock*, so Jesus Christ used a pun when he declared 'upon this rock I will build my church'.

There are also lots of puns in the history of English literature. A particularly moving one is from four hundred years ago when the poet John Donne was thrown into prison for marrying his sweetheart, Anne, without her father's permission. He summed up the experience: *John Donne, Anne Donne, Undone.*

ADVERBIAL PHRASES

An adverbial phrase provides more information about a verb. It answers three questions: **How? Where? When?** For example:

How did she do?	*She did <u>very well.</u>*
Where did you study?	*I studied <u>in the library</u>.*
When did you see him?	*I saw him <u>on Monday.</u>*

Test Yourself!

Underline the adverbial phrases in these sentences. Then check your answers on the next page.

1. I stepped onto the red carpet.

2. Put your homework on my desk!

3. The school's orchestra played quite brilliantly.

4. Before the lesson, I dropped my water bottle.

5. I'll study until I understand.

6. I promise to email you this evening.

7. The bird flew over my head.

8. During the performance, I fell asleep.

Joke Break
"We should tear down those hedges,'" said the man offensively.
"He didn't write a will," said the lawyer unwillingly.
"Your glasses are ready to collect," said the optician respectfully.

1. I stepped <u>onto the red carpet.</u>
2. Put your homework <u>on my desk!</u>
3. The school's orchestra played <u>quite brilliantly.</u>
4. <u>Before the lesson,</u> I dropped my water bottle.
5. I'll study <u>until I understand.</u>
6. I promise to email you <u>this evening.</u>
7. The bird flew <u>over my head.</u>
8. <u>During the performance,</u> I fell asleep.

WHAT'S THE DIFFERENCE BETWEEN A PREPOSITIONAL PHRASE AND AN ADVERBIAL PHRASE?

You might have noticed that some adverbial phrases begin with prepositions. This is because many adverbial phrases also function as prepositional phrases. There are differences, however:

1. A prepositional phrase begins with a preposition. It relates to an object, which might be a noun, pronoun or noun phrase. It doesn't refer to a subject. Examples:

> *on the fence*
> *on it*
> *on the wooden fence*

2. As we saw in the examples on the previous page, an adverbial phrase works **with** the verb. It answers the questions *How? Where?* or *When?* to provide more information about the verb itself.

WHY DO I NEED TO KNOW ABOUT ADVERBIAL PHRASES?

Like adverbs, adverbial phrases can add variety to your sentences. Study this example from *Alice's Adventures in Wonderland* by Lewis Carroll:

> [The Cheshire Cat] *vanished <u>quite slowly</u>, beginning with the end of the tail, and ending with the grin, which remained some time after the rest of it had gone.*

The adverbial phrase 'quite slowly' modifies and draws attention to the verb 'vanished'; the adverbial phrase surprises the reader because the act of vanishing is quick. The contradictory idea of vanishing slowly fits the author's style of playing with logic in a fantasy world, which is populated by talking animals.

Fascinating Fact!

Do you know the difference between *farther* and *further*? They both mean the same and are often used interchangeably. Generally speaking, *farther* references physical distance (it's easy to remember because it has the word *far* in it). For example: *I can walk farther than you.* We tend to use *further* when talking about abstract or metaphorical ideas. For example, *Without further ado, it's time for the next chapter. Do you have anything further to say? I do! Furthermore, I want to talk about simple and compound sentences!*

Chapter 12: Simple Sentences

This is a good sentence. It starts with a capital letter. It ends in a full stop. It's grammatically correct. We'll revise the grammar. Teachers like good grammar. You get marks for it. However, too many short sentences become boring. People like variety. I craft my sentences when I want to impress the examiner. I show off. My ideas uncurl on the page, slowly emerging. They stumble at first, like a reluctant teenager emerging from a bedroom at noon, and then they take hesitant steps, becoming stronger and stronger by the moment. Words, humming and buzzing, twisting and turning, begin to jostle for attention. Calmly, carefully, confidently, adverbs search for verbs, navigating through nifty nouns, chugging along with a smattering of inspiration. Hissing and spitting, sibilance becomes stronger, snaking along, pausing at commas, halting at full stops.

—Written by Kerry Lewis, inspired by Gary Provost

To boost your marks for punctuation and grammar, you need to vary your sentences. But how? We'll start by reviewing simple sentences. Then in subsequent chapters, we'll revise other sentence types.

HOW TO MAKE A SIMPLE SENTENCE

Let's review your knowledge of grammar so far. Answer the questions about this sentence: *She sits.*

1. **Who or what is the sentence about?** Answer: *She*. Therefore, *She* is the subject of the sentence.
2. **What does the subject do?** Answer: *sits*. Therefore, *sits* is the verb.
3. **Conclusion:** a simple sentence contains one subject and one verb.

Let's try this again. Answer the questions about this sentence: *He is sitting.*

1. **Who or what is the sentence about?** Answer: *He*. Therefore, *He* is the subject of the sentence.
2. **What does the subject do?** Answer: *is sitting*. Therefore, *is sitting* is a verb phrase.
3. **Conclusion:** a simple sentence contains one subject and either one verb or a verb phrase.

Grammar warning!
Simple sentences are often short; sometimes, however, they can have lots of adjectives and adverbs. For example: *The slimy, slithering, hissing snake coiled slowly around the broken lamppost.*

Even though this is a long sentence, there is still only one subject (*snake*) and one verb (*coiled*). Therefore, this is still a simple sentence.

Test Yourself!

Label the subject and verb or verb phrase in each of the sentences below. Then check your answers.

1. I shouted for help.

2. The icy wind knifed me without mercy.

3. The starless night was smothering me.

4. I staggered through the abandoned streets.

5. Wolves howled in unison.

6. I will be alone…

1. **I (subject)** *shouted (verb)* for help.
2. The icy **wind (subject)** *knifed(verb)* me without mercy.
3. The starless **night (subject)** *was smothering (verb phrase)* me.
4. **I (subject)** *staggered (verb)* through the abandoned streets.
5. **Wolves (subject)** *howled (verb)* in unison.
6. **I (subject)** *will be (verb phrase)* alone...

Fascinating Fact about the Space at the end of a Sentence!

When Johannes Gutenberg invented the printing press in the 15th century, it had movable, re-usable type (letters and punctuation marks). Today, his famous Gutenberg Bibles are worth about £3 million each.

Over time, rules about the space at the end of a sentence emerged. When the typewriter was invented in the late 19th century, typists used an earlier rule to recreate the idea of an enlarged space, by hitting the space bar twice to create a double space.

From the mid-twentieth century, editors of newspapers, magazines and books started to use a single space at the end of their sentences. Suddenly, whether to use a single or double space became a popular topic of discussion! Nowadays, the use of the single space is more popular.

WHY DO I NEED TO KNOW ABOUT SIMPLE SENTENCES?

Simple sentences often emphasise a particular thought or feeling. In this extract from *Persuasion* by Jane Austen, Lady Russell wants her friend Anne to visit Bath. The two simple sentences at the end of the extract emphasise her reasons:

Anne had been too little from home, too little seen. Her spirits were not high. A larger society would improve them.

A simple sentence can also hook a reader into a story by creating curiosity about what happens next. The first sentence of *Moby Dick* by Herman Melville is friendly, and he invites you to share his story:

Call me Ishmael. Some years ago—never mind how long precisely—having little or no money in my purse, and nothing particular to interest me on shore, I thought I would sail about a little and see the watery part of the world.

The phrase 'Call me' is a very informal way to introduce yourself, especially in 1851 when the book was published. It implies a casual attitude. This is developed when we read the second sentence and learn about his lifestyle as a drifter.

WHAT NEXT?

Next, we'll look at minor sentences. Before that, it's time for a...

Joke Break
We should never generalise.

Chapter 13: Minor Sentences

Yes, right. Really? The UK. And you? Sounds good. Best in the world. Absolutely. Got to go. Bye!

What do the above sentences have in common? They don't contain a subject and verb or verb phrase. They're therefore called minor sentences, and there are several types:

- **Exclamations and interjections:** *Oh! Really?*
- **Aphoristic expressions** (short sayings): *Better safe than sorry*
- **Answers to questions:** *No, thanks*
- **Self-identification:** *Peter, here.*
- **Noun phrases:** *a fearful man*
- **Vocatives** (used when talking to a person): Oi, *you!*

WHY DO I NEED TO KNOW ABOUT MINOR SENTENCES?

Minor sentences are an excellent way to focus the attention of the reader. Study this example paragraph from *Mr Bruff's Guide to GCSE English Language* (available on www.mrbruff.com). It deliberately uses minor sentences to introduce an essay:

Tired. Irritable. Unsociable. My 17-year-old brother is at his worst in the morning. Why? He has been up all night on Snapchat, Instagram and Twitter. Parents, teachers and politicians have voiced their concern about the negative impact these sites have on teenagers' lives: they believe that social networking sites should be banned. As a young person myself, I disagree.

In advertising campaigns today, minor sentences are often used in a similar way to emphasise points. Look out for them!

Minor sentences don't have to be single words. If a sentence is missing a subject or verb, it's still a minor sentence. Study this extract from Charles Dicken's *A Christmas Carol:*

Foggier yet, and colder. Piercing, searching, biting cold.

The first minor sentence freezes this moment in time, developing a sense of unease in the reader. The listing of adjectives in the second minor sentence builds momentum to focus on the importance of the cold which, we shortly learn, heralds the visitations of the four ghosts.

Minor sentences, as we saw in the introduction, can be noun phrases. In *A Christmas Carol*, Scrooge is visited by the ghost of his dead partner:

The same face: the very same. Marley in his pigtail, usual waistcoat, tights and boots; the tassels on the latter bristling, like his pigtail, and his coat-skirts, and the hair upon his head.

The minor sentences develop an impression of Marley as Scrooge sees him, building the horror that he is actually seeing a ghost.

Minor sentences or fragments therefore serve a range of purposes, and they're an effective way to vary your writing.

Joke Break
Minor sentences? Eliminate!

Chapter 14: Compound Sentences

A sentence walked into a school, and then it chatted to a friend.

Compound sentences are very easy to make: simply put two simple sentences together. For example: *She played football well, so her friends clapped.*

In a compound sentence, the simple sentences change their name to independent clauses. All compound sentences have two independent clauses, each with a subject and a verb or verb phrase.

COMPOUND SENTENCES WITH COORDINATING CONJUNCTIONS

In the example sentence above, the word *so* is a coordinating conjunction that acts like glue to stick the two independent clauses together. There are seven coordinating conjunctions, and an easy way to remember them is with the phrase **FANBOYS**: **F**or, **A**nd, **N**or, **B**ut, **O**r, **Y**et, **S**o. There's usually a comma before the conjunction. NB: if the compound sentence is very short, you can leave it out.

Test Yourself!

Make compound sentences by adding a coordinating conjunction (see FANBOYS, above). Use each word once. Then check your answers on the next page.

1. We ran out of money, _____ we went home early.

2. The sun came out, _____ everyone went to the beach.

3. Some students ate their lunch in the hall, _____ others enjoyed their lunch in the sunshine.

4. You can stay here, _____ you can go home!

5. She translated the page in no time at all, _____ she's fluent in two languages.

6. He doesn't like sweets, _____ does he like cake.

7. The snowstorm raged outside, _____ we were snug and warm by the fire.

WHY DO I NEED TO KNOW ABOUT COMPOUND SENTENCES?

Using compound sentences proves that you can vary your sentences. Read this example from Jane Austen's *Pride and Prejudice*:

> *He is a gentleman, and I am a gentleman's daughter. So far we are equal.*

The compound sentence creates a sense of balance, as the speaker Lizzie stresses the equality of her status with Mr Darcy (despite him being considerably richer than her). Note the simple sentence at the end for emphasis.

Shakespeare sometimes uses compound sentences to balance opposite ideas. In these examples, he reverses grammatical structure for artistic effect (this is known as chiasmus):

> *I wasted time, and now time doth waste me.*
> —*Richard II*
>
> *A fool thinks himself to be wise, but a wise man knows himself to be a fool.*
> —*As You Like It*

So does Alexandre Dumas:

> *All for one, and one for all!*
>
> —*The Three Musketeers*

Here, Shakespeare shocks his audience with ideas in the equally important independent clauses:

> *Hell is empty and all the devils are here.*
>
> —*The Tempest*

Samuel Johnson uses repetition at the start of the independent clauses (anaphora) for emphasis:

> *Every man has a right to utter what he thinks truth, and every other man has a right to knock him down for it.*
>
> —*The Life of Samuel Johnson* by James Boswell

Answers

1. We ran out of money, <u>so/and</u> we went home early.
2. The sun came out, <u>and/so</u> everyone went to the beach.
3. Some students ate their lunch in the hall, <u>but</u> others enjoyed their lunch in the sunshine.
4. You can stay here, <u>or</u> you can go home!
5. She translated the page in no time at all, <u>for</u> she's fluent in two languages.
6. He doesn't like sweets, <u>nor</u> does he like cake.
7. The snowstorm raged outside, <u>yet</u> we were snug and warm by the fire.

Test Yourself!

How good are you at identifying minor, simple and compound sentences? Read each sentence below and label the subject(s) and verb(s) or verb phrase(s). Then label the sentence.

Example: *I am drinking a lovely cup of coffee.* (subject: *I*, verb: *am drinking*—SIMPLE)

1. Sam drinks milk.

2. Sam drinks milk, and Jo drinks tea.

3. Delicious!

4. The silver moon is hiding behind the dark clouds.

5. Ahmed is writing a lot, but he isn't checking his work.

6. You can have a healthy carrot stick, or you can eat a huge mountain of chocolate.

7. The tall, fearless, blonde-haired girl walked slowly into the dark, forbidding, haunted house.

8. Oh, no!

9. My father offered me some money, so I washed his car.

10. The girls were tired, yet they played football.

1. Sam drinks milk. (subject: *Sam*, verb: *drinks*—SIMPLE)
2. Sam drinks milk, and Jo drinks tea. (subjects: *Sam* and *Jo*, verbs: *drinks* and *drinks*—COMPOUND)
3. Delicious! (No subject, no verb—MINOR)
4. The silver moon is hiding behind the dark clouds. (subject: *moon*, verb phrase: *is hiding*—SIMPLE)
5. Ahmed is writing a lot, but he isn't checking his work. (subjects: *Ahmed* and *he*, verb phrases: *is writing* and *isn't checking*—COMPOUND)
6. You can have a healthy carrot stick, or you can eat a huge mountain of chocolate. (subjects: *you* and *you*, verb phrases: *can have* and *can eat*—COMPOUND)
7. The tall, fearless, blonde-haired girl walked slowly into the dark, forbidding, haunted house. (subject: *girl*, verb: *walked*—SIMPLE)
8. My father offered me some money, so I washed his car. (subjects: *father* and *I*, verbs: *offered* and *washed*—COMPOUND)
9. Oh, no! (No subject, no verb—MINOR)
10. The girls were tired, yet they played football. (subjects: the *girls* and *they*, verbs: *were* and *played*—COMPOUND)

Fascinating Fact!

There's a common belief that you can't put the coordinating conjunctions *and, but* or *so* at the beginning of a sentence.

Interestingly, there are no grammatical foundations for this because many historical literary texts have sentences that begin with coordinating conjunctions. In *The Pardoner's Tale* in *The Canterbury Tales*, Geoffrey Chaucer writes: 'And right anon thanne comen tombesteres', which translates as 'And right away then come dancing girls'. Moreover, Bishop Lowth, a famous eighteenth-century author of grammar textbooks, began lots of his sentences with *and*.

So where did this rule come from? There's a theory that teachers in the nineteenth century noticed how pupils were overusing *and, but* or *so* at the start of their sentences. So, what did they do? They banned it!

COMPOUND SENTENCES WITH SEMICOLONS

To create an elegant looking compound sentence, try replacing a coordinating conjunction with a semicolon. For example:

> She played football well, and her friends clapped.
> She played football well; her friends clapped.

This works better with *so, and, but*. Here are more examples:

> He was tired, so he went to bed early.
> He was tired; he went to bed early.
>
> I checked my homework, and there were hardly any errors.
> I checked my homework; there were hardly any errors.

> She likes chocolate, but her brother prefers crisps.
> She likes chocolate; her brother prefers crisps.

It's easy, isn't it? This is a great way to showcase your advanced punctuation skills. Now let's move it up a level!

Joke Break
When Santa and his wife split up, their divorce lawyers gave them a semicolon.
Semicolons are great for separating independent clauses.

COMPOUND SENTENCES WITH SEMICOLONS AND TRANSITION WORDS (CONJUNCTIVE ADVERBS)

A transition word, also known as a *conjunctive adverb*, shows how ideas relate to one another. Common transition words are:

Accordingly	Indeed	Nonetheless
Also	Instead	Similarly
Besides	Likewise	Still
Certainly	Meanwhile	Subsequently
Consequently	Moreover	Then
Finally	Namely	Thereafter
Further	Now	Therefore
Furthermore	Otherwise	Thus
Hence	Nevertheless	Undoubtedly
However	Next	

Smarten your compound sentences with a semicolon, transition word and then a comma. Examples:

> I catch the bus to school; *however,* my brother prefers to walk.
> That huge dog is frightening; *accordingly,* I'm keeping my distance.
> I played tennis; *meanwhile,* my friend was eating strawberries.
> I studied in credibly hard for the test; *consequently,* I passed with 98%.
> I endured the first half hour of a boring film; *finally,* I turned off the television.

Common Mistakes with Transition Words

As we have seen, transition words can be used with a semicolon and a comma to join two independent clauses in a compound sentence. They can be used in other ways, too. What's wrong with these sentences? Check your answers on the next page.

1. At 8 o'clock, Suzie was supposed to be walking to school. However she was still eating her breakfast.

2. At 8 o'clock, Suzie was supposed to be walking to school. She was however still eating her breakfast.

3. At 8 o'clock, Suzie was supposed to be walking to school. She was still eating her breakfast however.

Study how the commas are used:

1. At 8 o'clock, Suzie was supposed to be walking to school. However, she was still eating her breakfast.
2. At 8 o'clock, Suzie was supposed to be walking to school. She was, however, still eating her breakfast.
3. At 8 o'clock, Suzie was supposed to be walking to school. She was still eating her breakfast, however.

NB: If the transition word is between a subject and verb, no comma is needed. Examples:

> Andrew worked all day. He *then* went home.
> Andrew worked all day. He *subsequently* went home.

Test Yourself!

Study the chart on the previous page. Then write a transition word to complete each sentence, below. Include a semicolon and/or comma(s) if needed. check your answers on the next page.

1. I like chocolate. My sister prefers sweets _____.
2. You need to learn your spelling corrections _____ you'll repeat the same mistakes.
3. I go shopping every Saturday. My friends _____ like shopping.
4. I practised the piano every day _____ I failed the exam.
5. Mark is brilliant at maths. He is _____ a top mathematician.
6. She was busy cleaning the house. Her husband _____ was watching television.
7. They are getting married next March. _____ they are honeymooning in Greece.
8. Karim ditched his girlfriend. A year later, she _____ loves him.
9. She created a revision timetable and stuck to it. _____ she passed the exam.
10. He was spotted by a talent scout _____ a star was born.

Joke Break
If my colon is removed in an operation, will I be left with a semicolon?

Fascinating Fact!

If you don't use a comma with *however* at the beginning of a sentence, it affects the meaning of the sentence. For example:

> *However* hard you try, it won't make a difference.
> *However* beautiful you think your garden is, mine is better.
> *However* you look at it, you'll find nothing wrong.

With the above examples, *however* means *no matter how*. It's an adverb, not a transition word.

1. I like chocolate. My sister prefers sweets, <u>however/instead.</u>
2. You need to learn your spelling corrections; <u>otherwise</u>, you'll repeat the same mistakes.
3. I go shopping every Saturday. My friends <u>also</u> like shopping.
4. I practised the piano every day; <u>nevertheless/however</u>, I failed the exam.
5. Mark is brilliant at maths. He is <u>undoubtedly/certainly/consequently/accordingly/</u> a top mathematician.
6. She was busy cleaning the house. Her husband, <u>meanwhile/however,</u> was watching television.
7. They are getting married next March. <u>Furthermore</u>, they are honeymooning in Greece.
8. Karim ditched his girlfriend. A year later, she <u>still</u> loves him.
9. She created a revision timetable and stuck to it. <u>Therefore/consequently/hence/subsequently</u>, she passed the exam.
10. He was spotted by a talent scout; <u>thus/consequently/hence</u>, a star was born.

COMPOUND SENTENCES WITH COLONS

Use a colon to join two independent clauses when the second clause develops the idea of the first. I like to think of the colon as a fanfare of trumpets, heralding something important. For example:

> I have something to say: you're fired!
> The reason you won the race is simple: you trained hard.

Test Yourself!

Use the four ways of making compound sentences to join the independent clauses. You might have to add words; sometimes, more than one answer is possible. Then check your answers.

1. I went to the field. I played football.

2. I forgot one important detail. I hadn't written my name on the exam paper.

3. Tom hates doing homework. He understands that it's important.

4. I listen to rock music. My friends hate it.

5. She wanted to watch another Mr Bruff YouTube video. I helped her to find the website link.

6. Charlie bought his sister a bracelet. It was her birthday.

7. The students went to a revision lesson. It was very useful.

8. Some of my friends went to a Model United Nations conference. They were invited to speak!

9. Molly loves watching YouTube videos. She decided to become a YouTuber.

10. The student needed help with her homework. She asked a friend.

Fascinating Fact!

Read this sentence, which is from *The Four Oxen and the Lion* by the ancient Greek storyteller Aesop. He wrote it two thousand, six hundred years ago:

> *United we stand, divided we fall.*

It should have a semicolon, but they hadn't been invented.

Suggested answers are below; more than one answer might be possible.

1. I went to the field, and I played football.
2. I forgot one important detail: I hadn't written my name on the exam paper.
3. Tom hates doing homework; however, he understands that it's important.
4. I listen to rock music, but my friends hate it.
5. She wanted to watch another Mr Bruff YouTube video, so I helped her to find the website link.
6. Charlie bought his sister a bracelet; it was her birthday.
7. The students went to a revision lesson; it was very useful.
8. Some of my friends went to a Model United Nations conference: they were invited to speak!
9. Molly loves watching YouTube videos; therefore, she decided to become a YouTuber.
10. The student needed help with her homework; she asked a friend.

Common Mistake: Confusion between the Colon and Semicolon

Compare these sentences which have identical words. The punctuation subtly alters the meaning:

> He locked himself in his room; his girlfriend had ditched him.
> He locked himself in his room: his girlfriend had ditched him.

With the first example, the semicolon divides two independent clauses, and they have equal importance. It's like drifting into a classroom, nodding casually at a few friends, then drifting into another and nodding at a few more.

With the second sentence, the colon introduces something far more important than the man locking himself in his room. Ah, yes...DRAMATIC PAUSE, FANFARE OF TRUMPETS AND ROLL OF DRUMS...his girlfriend has DITCHED him!

USE OF COORDINATING CONJUNCTIONS IN LITERATURE

We have seen that coordinating conjunctions (FANBOYS) join two independent clauses that are equally weighted in importance. They can also be used to join grammatically equal or similar words, phrases or clauses. In this extract from *Dombey and Son*, Charles Dickens uses coordinating conjunctions to recreate the excitement of the child:

> *'He knows all about the deep sea, and the fish that are in it, and the great monsters that come and lie on rocks in the sun, and dive into the water again when they're startled, blowing and splashing so, that they can be heard for miles. There are some creatures', said Paul, warming with his subject, 'I don't know how many yards long, and I forget their names, but Florence knows, that pretend to be in distress; and when a man goes near them, out of compassion, they open their great jaws, and attack him.'*

WHAT NEXT?

Well done! You've studied compound sentences, coordinating conjunctions and how the colon and semicolon can be used to enhance meaning. Let's finish this chapter with a joke:

> **Joke Break**
> **QUESTION:** What happened when the semicolon broke some grammar laws?
> **ANSWER:** It was given two consecutive sentences.

Chapter 15: Complex Sentences

> A complex sentence walked into a school while checking its phone.
> While checking its phone, a complex sentence walked into a school.

WHAT'S A COMPLEX SENTENCE?

A complex sentence contains a main clause and at least one subordinate clause. For example:

Rushing the test, he finished too early.

↑   ↑

subordinate   *main clause*
clause

The main clause looks like a simple sentence because it has a subject and verb or verb phrase. In a complex sentence, the simple sentence changes its name to a main clause. The bit that's left over doesn't make sense by itself—this is called a subordinate clause or a dependent clause.

Subordinate means less important, and some sentences have more than one, as we shall see in the next chapter. A subordinate clause depends upon the main clause.

Joke Break
Question: What do you call Santa's little helpers?
Answer: Subordinate clauses.

There are three ways to form a subordinate clause, and you've studied the first two in earlier chapters.

1. SUBORDINATING CLAUSES WITH NON-FINITE VERB

In a subordinate clause, a non-finite verb stays the same, regardless of the other words around it. There are three non-finite verb forms—you might recognise some as verb phrases.

The present participle -ing

If you need to revise the present participle, see **chapter 6: verbs**. Here are some example subordinate clauses that use the present participle:

Rushing **the test,** he finished too early.
He finished too early, *rushing* **the test.**

Drinking **the water,** she quenched her thirst.
She quenched her thirst, *drinking* **the water.**

Joke Break
Ah, dear! Simple sentences, minor sentences, compound sentences...They're all so complex to me.

Common Mistake

> Some people forget to use a comma to divide the main and subordinate clauses. Remember:
>
> A cat has claws at the end of its paws,
> A comma's a pause at the end of a clause!

The past participle -ed

The past participle shows a completed action in the past (it's the simple past tense form of a verb, see **chapters 6 and 7)**. Example subordinate clauses using past participles:

> *Questioned* **by the police,** the prisoner admitted his guilt.
> *Picked* **only this morning,** the strawberries tasted delicious.

The infinitive to + verb

You might remember that we debated whether to split infinitives in **chapter 6.** Example subordinate clauses using infinitives:

> *To pass* **my exams,** I should create a revision timetable.
> I should create a revision timetable *to pass* **my exams.**

You don't usually need a comma with the infinitive after the main clause. However…

Fascinating Fact!

In the first sentence of *A Christmas Carol*, Charles Dickens deliberately uses a comma: *Marley was dead, to begin with.* The comma invites the reader to pause and to reflect on the infinitive, which suggests that Marley will not remain dead. This hooks the reader by introducing the theme of the supernatural.

2. SUBORDINATING CLAUSES WITH RELATIVE PRONOUN + FINITE VERB

You might remember relative pronouns from chapter 8. A finite verb has a subject or an implied subject. Reminder: you need a comma with relative clauses only if you're adding extra information:

> There are lots of students *who* **love English lessons.**
> That's Karim, *who* **happens to be in my class.**
> This is a GCSE revision guide, *which* **was written by Mr Bruff.**
> This is <u>the</u> GCSE revision guide *which* **was written by Mr Bruff.**

Test Yourself!

Underline the subordinate clauses in the following sentences. Then check your answers.

1. Peering through the fog, we could see nothing.

2. Watered once a week, your plants will thrive.

3. I should read more to broaden my vocabulary.

4. I'll tell you who he is.

5. These are the jeans which I lost.

1. <u>Peering through the fog,</u> we could see nothing.
2. <u>Watered once a week,</u> your plants will thrive.
3. I should read more <u>to broaden my vocabulary.</u>
4. I'll tell you <u>who he is.</u>
5. These are the jeans <u>which I lost.</u>

3. SUBORDINATE CLAUSES WITH SUBORDINATING CONJUNCTION + FINITE VERB

A subordinating conjunction is any conjunction that is not a coordinating (FANBOYS) conjunction. Here are some common subordinating conjunctions that form subordinate clauses:

After	Because	Once	Until
Although	Before	Only if	Whatever
As	By the time	Provided that	When
As if	Even if	Since	Whenever
As long as	Even though	Than	Whereas
As much as	If	That	Wherever
As soon as	In order that/to	Though	Whether
As though	In case	Unless	While

Now read the example sentences. Note that there is a comma only if the sentence begins with a subordinating conjunction:

Until you get home, I'll wait.
I'll wait *until* you get home.

Test Yourself!

Complete the following sentences with a subordinating conjunction. Sometimes, more than one answer is possible. Check your answers on the next page.

1. I've started to do this exercise _____ I don't really feel like working.

2. I'll go out with you_____ you pay!

3. It'll be Christmas _____ I've finished.

4. I wonder _____ I'll win the lottery.

5. My Mum will take me to a theme park _____ I pass my exams.

6. She won't make plans _____ I get my exam results.

7. I won't pass my exams _____ I start to work.

8. I'd better pay more attention _____ my teacher won't be happy.

9. This is quite interesting _____you settle down to it...

10. Now we have to stop _____ I've hardly started!

It's interesting to consider how meaning changes if more than one answer is possible:

1. I've started to do this exercise <u>even though/although/though/</u> I don't really feel like working.
2. I'll go out with you <u>as long as/if/only if/provided that/whenever</u> you pay!
3. It'll be Christmas <u>by the time/when</u> I've finished.
4. I wonder <u>if</u> I'll win the lottery.
5. My Mum will take me to a theme park <u>after/as long as/as soon as/if/only if/provided that/when</u> I pass my exams.
6. She won't make plans <u>till/until/before</u> I get my exam results.
7. I won't pass my exams <u>unless/until/(even if)</u> I start to work.
8. I'd better pay more attention <u>since/because</u> my teacher won't be happy.
9. This is quite interesting <u>when/once</u> you settle down to it...
10. Now we have to stop <u>although/though/even though</u> I've hardly started!

Common Mistake

In the above exercise, you might have written: *also, however, next, meanwhile, then* or *finally*. A reminder that these are transition words or conjunctive adverbs (see **chapter 14, Compound Sentences**). They're not subordinating conjunctions.

Fascinating Fact!

There are some archaic (old-fashioned) conjunctions that we don't use any more; you might come across them with Shakespeare or other older texts:

CONJUNCTION	MEANING	EXAMPLE SENTENCE
LEST	in case	*Let go thy hold when a great wheel runs down a hill, **lest** it break thy neck with following it... —King Lear*
WHEREFORE	why	*O Romeo, Romeo! **Wherefore** art thou Romeo? —Romeo and Juliet*
WHEREOF	of which	*...my body to the earth **whereof** it is made —Shakespeare's will.*

REVISION: IDENTIFYING AND NON-IDENTIFYING EMBEDDED CLAUSES

You now know how to vary your sentences with three types of subordinate clause. In chapter 8, we looked at embedded subordinate clauses. This is when you take a main clause, split it in half and insert a subordinate clause. For example:

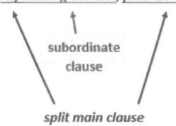

In the same chapter, we studied how you might use commas with an embedded subordinate clause to show that you're adding unessential information. For example:

> Erin, who's going to the party, scored full marks in the maths exam.

The commas are similar to brackets, creating a non-identifying or drop-in clause. The main meaning of the sentence is: *Erin scored full marks in the maths exam.* If we wanted to, we could delete the subordinate clause.

Now read the same sentence with no commas:

| **Question:** | I know two Erins. Which Erin scored full marks in her maths exam? |
| **Answer:** | *Erin who's going to the party scored full marks in the maths exam.* |

The absence of commas means that the embedded subordinate clause is an identifying clause. It identifies that the Erin who scored full marks in her maths exam is the same Erin who is going to the party (as opposed to another Erin who isn't going to the party). We cannot delete the subordinate clause because it's essential to understanding the sentence.

COMPLEX SENTENCES IN LITERATURE

If you're feeling philosophical, here are some famous sentences in literature:

Men of sense, whatever you may choose to say, do not want silly wives.
—*Emma,* Jane Austen

If a man does not keep pace with his companions, perhaps it is because he hears a different drummer.
—*Walden,* Henry David Thoreau

The path to my fixed purpose is laid on iron rails on which my soul is grooved to run.
—*Moby Dick,* Herman Melville

Whatever our souls are made of, his and mine are the same.
—*Wuthering Heights,* Emily Bronte

If you look for perfection, you'll never be content.
—*Anna Karenina,* Leo Tolstoy

Fascinating Fact!

This sentence doesn't appear to make sense:

The mouse the cat the dog chased killed ate the cheese.

It's confusing because it has multiple embedded defining clauses. This might help you to understand:
- *The mouse ate the cheese* is a split main clause.
- The cat then killed the mouse—*the cat killed* is a split subordinate clause (*The mouse the cat killed ate the cheese*)
- The cat had been chased by the dog.

The grammar of the sentence is correct but stylistically weak!

WHAT NEXT?

Let's examine some better multi-clause sentences!

Chapter 16: Multi-clause Sentences

Complex sentences might have one subordinate clause or multiple subordinate clauses or phrases. This example has two embedded subordinate clauses:

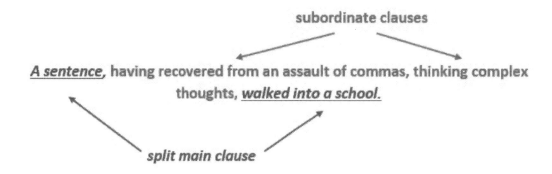

In this chapter, we'll explore ways to create your own multi-clause sentences.

EXPERIMENTING WITH MULTI-CLAUSE SENTENCES

Embedded subordinate clauses

Try embedding a couple of subordinate clauses like the example above. If you're not sure whether you're putting the subordinate clauses in the right place, delete them. What's left should be grammatically correct. To use the introductory example, *A sentence walked into a school.*

Build on fronted adverbial phrases

A fronted adverbial is a word or phrase that begins a sentence and describes the action that follows. We saw in **Chapter 11: Adverbs** how adverbs can be used to begin sentences. For example:

Nervously, the job applicant answered the questions.

Nervously is a fronted adverbial. Try adding a subordinate clause to make a multi-clause sentence:

Nervously, stuttering badly, the job applicant answered the questions.

In the next examples, the fronted adverbials are in italics, and the subordinate clauses are underlined:

Quite understandably, drinking the water, she quenched her thirst.
Earlier this morning, questioned by the police, the prisoner admitted his guilt.
Now, to pass my exams, I should create a revision timetable.
In this school, there are lots of students who love English lessons.
Occasionally, I'll wait until you get home.

Put the main clause at the end

Try using multiple clauses or phrases, placing the subject at the end of a sentence:

Every night, after the church clock chimed 12, scuttling and creeping, snuffling, whirring and clicking, came the creatures of darkness.

EXAMPLES IN LITERATURE

Multi-clause sentences can develop:
- Mood: atmosphere that's created by the way the writer describes the setting
- Tone: the emotions that the writer makes the reader feel

Let's study some examples by Charles Dickens. The main clauses are in **bold**.

1. *A Tale of Two Cities*

*A dream, all a dream, that ends in nothing, and leaves the sleeper where he lay down, but **I wish you to know** that you inspired it.*

The phrases and clauses build momentum, developing a tone of yearning and despair. The main clause attempts to break this tone by creating a connection with the listener.

2. *Great Expectations*

***I loved her against reason**, against promise, against peace, against hope, against happiness, against all discouragement that could be.*

Here, the main clause at the beginning introduces a more rational tone, as the speaker understands the impossibility of his love being returned. The prepositional phrases build momentum to emphasise his point.

WHAT NEXT?

We'll finish this chapter with a question:

What do you get when you cross a compound sentence with a complex sentence?

The answer in in the next chapter.

Chapter 17: Compound-Complex Sentences

Congratulations! So far, we've revised simple sentences, minor sentences, compound sentences and types of complex sentence. This chapter reviews our final sentence type, which is the compound-complex sentence. A compound-complex sentence contains a compound sentence of two independent clauses and at least one subordinate clause. These clauses can be arranged in different ways. Study the examples below.

Example 1:

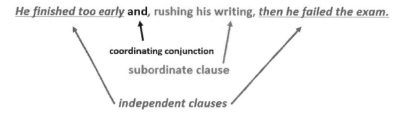

He finished too early, **and** *then he failed the exam,* rushing his writing.

coordinating conjunction

independent clauses

subordinate clause

Example 2:

Rushing his writing, *he finished too early,* **and** *then he failed the exam.*

subordinate clause

coordinating conjunction

independent clauses

Example 3a:

He finished too early, rushing his writing, **and** *then he failed the exam.*

coordinating conjunction

subordinate clause

independent clauses

Example 3b:

He finished too early **and,** rushing his writing, *then he failed the exam.*

coordinating conjunction

subordinate clause

independent clauses

Example 3c

He finished too early **and** *then,* rushing his writing, *he failed the exam.*

(adverb)

coordinating conjunction

subordinate clause

independent clauses

With the last example, 'then' is an adverb, which doesn't affect the grammar. With all the examples, the positioning of the subordinate clause subtly affects emphasis and meaning. In the first example, the subordinate clause is an afterthought; in the second, it's the main focus of the sentence. In the final example, the subordinate clause builds up to the final part of the sentence, and the placement of the adverb affects the speaker's tone. In literature, compound-complex sentences can have multiple subordinate clauses and/or phrases. Let's examine some literary examples, breaking the sentence parts down. The independent clauses are underlined and in italics.

COMPOUND-COMPLEX SENTENCES IN LITERATURE

Example 1:

He stepped down, trying not to look long at her, as if* she were the sun, **yet** *he saw her*, like the sun, even without looking.

—*Anna Karenina*, Leo Tolstoy

*NB: The phrase beginning 'as if' serves as a simile, not a coordinating conjunction.

The independent clauses focus on commonplace actions while the multiple phrases and subordinate clauses focus the reader's attention on the similes, which reveal how she dazzles him. The compound-complex sentence therefore heightens the contrast between everyday actions and the the impact that she has on him, revealing the intensity of his love.

Example 2:

Authors often use long sentences with multiple clauses or phrases to develop atmosphere or mood:

To see the dingy cloud come drooping down, obscuring everything, *one might have thought that Nature lived hard by*, **and** *was brewing* * *on a large scale*.

—*A Christmas Carol*, Charles Dickens

* When a verb in a compound sentence shares the same subject (in this case, 'Nature'), there is no need to repeat the subject.

The subordinate clauses mirror the fog creeping up slowly, creating an uneasy, supernatural mood. The fog is so thick that it's 'obscuring everything'; this might be a metaphor for Scrooge's inability to see the consequences of his actions. The 'dingy' and 'drooping' cloud of fog has murky connotations and develops a sense of Scrooge being approached by something that he cannot see, something beyond his control. The independent clauses focus on the personification of Nature, which is like a witch 'brewing' spells on 'a large scale'; this develops the uneasy mood, as we associate witches with evil, so we know that Scrooge will experience unpleasantness. The 'brewing' imagery foreshadows (gives hints of) Scrooge's ghostly visitors.

Example 3:

This is a description of finding a child with his head stuck in some railings:

I made my way to the poor child, who was one of the dirtiest little unfortunates I ever saw, **and** *found* * *him very hot and frightened and crying loudly*, fixed by the neck between two iron railings, while a milkman and a beadle, with the kindest intentions possible, were endeavouring to drag him back by the legs, under a general impression that his skull was compressible by those means.

—*Bleak House*, Charles Dickens

* The verb in the compound sentence shares the same subject—'I'—so there is no need to repeat the subject.

The subordinate clauses and phrases develop the focus on the incompetent actions of the milkman and beadle, creating humour for the Victorian reader.

WHAT NEXT?

We've looked at coordinating and subordinating conjunctions. They make a fascinating pair…

Chapter 18: Paired (or Correlative) Conjunctions

I once went on a date with a girl called Simile. I don't know what I metaphor.

The introductory joke contains puns on the words *simile* and *metaphor*. It's a lesser known fact that the simile *as…as* are paired (or correlative) conjunctions:

My brother (noun) is **as** *tall* (adjective) **as** my *father* (noun).
My reluctant friend (noun) walks **as** *slowly* (adverb) **as** a *snail* (noun).

PAIRED (OR CORRELATIVE) CONJUNCTIONS

Other paired conjunctions are in **bold**, below. Paired conjunctions are always used with the same parts of speech, which might be pairs of nouns, verbs, prepositions, etc. For example:

I'll have **both** the *dessert* (noun) **and** the *coffee* (noun).
I'm on a diet **not** *for* (preposition) my boyfriend **but** *for* (preposition) me.
My teacher **not only** *requires* (verb) my homework **but also** *wants* (verb) it to be good.
This evening, I can **either** *start* (verb) my English homework or *do* (verb) maths.

Test Yourself!

Write one of these pairs of conjunctions in the sentences below. Then check your answers on the next page.

both … and	either … or	not…but
whether…or	neither … nor	not only…but also

1. I'm _____ interested _____ bored.

2. I can't decide _____ to apply to university _____ to look for a job.

3. The film is _____ witty _____ funny.

4. I have found _____ a purse in the attic, _____ a £20 note!

5. I'll _____ catch a bus, _____ I'll walk home.

6. I'm disappointed _____ by your behaviour _____ by your attitude.

Fascinating Fact! Literary Lifestyle Advice

Here's some advice that Polonius in Shakespeare's *Hamlet* gives his son, using paired conjunctions:

Neither a borrower nor a lender be;
For loan oft loses both itself and friend,
And borrowing dulls the edge of husbandry.

This very roughly translates as: *Don't borrow or lend anyone any money. If you lend money to a friend who doesn't pay it back, you'll lose both the money and your friend. If you borrow from others, you won't be good at budgeting and managing your finances.* Sensible advice!

1. I'm <u>neither</u> interested <u>nor</u> bored.
2. I can't decide <u>whether</u> to apply to university <u>or</u> to look for a job.
3. The film is <u>both</u> witty <u>and</u> funny.
4. I have found <u>not only</u> a purse in the attic <u>but also</u> a £20 note!
5. I'll <u>either</u> catch a bus, <u>or</u> I'll walk home.
6. I'm disappointed <u>not</u> by your behaviour <u>but</u> by your attitude.

PUNCTUATION RULE

We don't have a comma with paired conjunctions unless (as with question 5, above) the comma separates two independent clauses in a compound sentence. Use commas to insert a subordinate clause (e.g. *Neither the chicken, which looks overcooked and greasy, nor the ham is tempting*). So why isn't it *are tempting*? After all, 1 chicken + 1 ham = 2 types of food. Let's review the grammar!

GRAMMAR

Rule 1: Singular and plural subjects—verb agreement

In chapter 6, we looked at subject-verb agreement. As you already know, a subject *does* the verb. With paired conjunctions, there are two subjects. If there's a singular subject and a plural subject, the verb always agrees with the second subject. Examples:

> Every day, **either** my daughter **or** my *sons give* me a hug.
> **Not only** our sons **but also** our *daughter needs* new clothes.
> **Neither** my pen **nor** my *pencils are* anywhere to be found.

Exception: With *both...and*, the verb is always plural. Example: <u>*Both Bryn and Aron like* the same girl.</u>

Rule 2: Noun and pronoun agreement

If a pronoun is used, it also agrees with the second noun. For example: *Neither my sister nor my <u>brothers</u> like <u>their</u> lunch.*

Test Yourself!

How well do you understand these rules? Read the sentences and circle the correct verb or pronoun. Then check your answers on the next page.

1. Neither my keys nor my bag <u>is/are</u> where I left them.

2. Whether she goes or they all <u>goes/go</u> is up to you.

3. Either Italy or the Greek islands <u>is/are</u> a great holiday destination.

4. Not only Paul but also Mary <u>is/are</u> going to the concert.

5. Not only my pet rabbit but my hamsters <u>eat/eats</u> carrots in small portions.

6. Both my dad and my brother <u>relaxes/relax</u> with a book in the evening.

7. Neither my parents nor my uncle <u>eats/eat</u> <u>his/their</u> five-a-day.

8. Both my little sister, who is adorable, and my baby brother, who cries at night, <u>loves/love</u> mum.

9. Neither my cat nor my dogs <u>likes/like</u> the taste of <u>its/their</u> stale water.

10. I don't know whether your girlfriend, whom I don't know very well, <u>has/have</u> decided to go to the party.

1. Neither my keys nor my bag <u>is</u> where I left them.
2. Whether she goes or they all <u>go</u> is up to you.
3. Either Italy or the Greek islands <u>are</u> a great holiday destination.
4. Not only Paul but also Mary <u>is</u> going to the concert.
5. Not only my pet rabbit but my hamsters <u>eat</u> carrots in small portions.
6. Both my dad and my brother <u>relax</u> with a book in the evening.
7. Neither my parents nor my uncle <u>eats</u> <u>his</u> five-a-day.
8. Both my little sister, who is adorable, and my baby brother, who cries at night, <u>adore</u> my mum.
9. Neither my cat nor my dogs <u>like</u> the taste of <u>their</u> stale water.
10. I don't know whether your girlfriend, whom I don't know very well, <u>has</u> decided to go to the party.

With question 10, here's a handy tip: delete the subordinate clause. This should leave you with *girlfriend…has*, which is good subject-verb agreement.

Joke Break

Question: What advice does a bank manager give a new customer?
Answer: Neither a borrower nor a spender be.

SUMMARY OF CONJUNCTIONS

Well done! You have finished studying the three types of conjunctions:

1. Paired (or correlative) conjunctions, explained in this chapter.
2. Co-ordinating conjunctions, used in compound sentences (*for, and, nor, but, or, yet, so*).
3. Subordinating conjunctions, which introduce subordinate clauses. These are all other conjunctions, for example, *because, if, before, after*, etc.

Let's end this chapter by celebrating with some conjunctions jokes:

Joke Break

Grunt the caveman is inventing language.
   He runs up to his friend with great excitement and says, "I've just invented conjunctions!"
   His friend replies, "So?"

There's a school in Grammarland where conjunctions are banned. No *ifs* or *buts* about it.

Definition of *conjunctionitis:*
An illness characterised by the creation of extremely long 'sentences' that contain too many conjunctions.

The final joke leads us nicely into our next chapter.

A comma suffering from *conjunctionitis* walks into a school and then it has a drink of lemonade and then it leaves and it trips up on its way out and it gets up but it loses its way and then it finally manages to leave and then it goes home.

A comma splice walks into a school, it drinks a glass of lemonade, it leaves, it trips up on its way out, then it gets up, it loses its way, then it finally manages to leave, then it goes home.

What's wrong with the introductory paragraphs? In the first example, there are too many conjunctions. The student's ideas are running away with themselves. These are called runaway sentences or run-on sentences. In the second sentence, there are commas instead of full stops—this is called comma splicing.

Imagine your exhausted but devoted English teacher, red-eyed and yawning, marking your homework at midnight. It's taken several hours so far. Yours is the final book in what was a mountainous pile— the size of Everest. Your work contains sentences like the ones above.

You are now going to experience what it's like to be a teacher.

Test Yourself—Runaway Sentences!

Read the advice below, which contains useful information about how to cope with exam-related stress. Add capital letters, full stops and commas where necessary. You might have to delete words. Then check your answers on the next page.

How to cope with stress: part 1

Stress in the build-up to exams is quite common many students become stressed when they are preparing for exams but a realistic revision timetable will give them more control and the timetable should include breaks because these are a good way to unwind

If you become stressed don't get stressed about it and most importantly stay away from negative stressful people and they'll make you worse and try not to compare how much you've done with your friends because everybody's different

Some students by experimenting with ways to calm themselves down stop their negative thoughts and they might take deep breaths or they might play mental games to distract themselves

Stress in the build-up to exams is quite common. Many students become stressed when they are preparing for exams, but a realistic revision timetable will give them more control. The timetable should include breaks because these are a good way to unwind.

If you become stressed, don't get stressed about it. Most importantly, stay away from negative, stressful people. They'll make you worse. Try not to compare how much you've done with your friends because everybody's different.

Some students, by experimenting with ways to calm themselves down, stop their negative thoughts. They might take deep breaths, or they might play mental games to distract themselves.

Test Yourself—Spliced Commas!

Now read the rest of the advice sheet, which is full of spliced commas. Again, add capital letters and full stops. **Some commas need deleting but, if they separate clauses, you'll need to keep them.** Check your answers on the next page.

How to cope with stress, part 2

Another strategy that successful students use is to think about something that makes them happy, this calms them down, by telling themselves they CAN do well, they become more positive.

Successful students also look after themselves, they eat a good breakfast, especially on the morning of an exam, many people take a banana to school because it's a better source of energy than chocolate, they eat a banana before they go in the exam room, which helps them to concentrate for longer.

Exercise is good for stress, you should also sleep regular hours, so never revise in bed, associating bed with a good night's sleep, rather than revision, is much better for your stress levels.

Some students, after following this advice, still need help, if you are one of them, you must talk to someone, if friends or family are unable to help, call ChildLine on 0800 1111.

Fascinating Fact!
In 2010, some writing that had been hidden for 350 years behind a monument was discovered on a wall of the magnificent Salisbury Cathedral in Wiltshire. Experts believe that it had been written a hundred years earlier, making it nearly 500 years old.
At that time, it was against the law to translate the Bible from Latin into English—this theory might explain why the writing was kept from sight. Unfortunately, no-one can read what it says. The moral? Always check your work.

Another strategy that successful students use is to think about something that makes them happy. This calms them down. By telling themselves they CAN do well, they become more positive.

Successful students also look after themselves. They eat a good breakfast, especially on the morning of an exam. Many people take a banana to school because it's a better source of energy than chocolate. They eat a banana before they go in the exam room, which helps them to concentrate for longer.

Exercise is good for stress. You should also sleep regular hours, so never revise in bed. Associating bed with a good night's sleep, rather than revision, is much better for your stress levels.

Some students, after following this advice, still need help. If you are one of them, you must talk to someone. If friends or family are unable to help, call ChildLine on 0800 1111.

Fascinating Fact! The Oxford Comma

There's a punctuation mark called the Oxford comma. Its name comes from Oxford University Press, where it was used by its editors and printers. It's rarely used in the UK, being much more common in America.

The Oxford comma is used with *and* or *or* before the last item of a list. For example: *I bought some bananas, apples, tomatoes, and plums. I don't like chicken, ham, or sausages.*

In the UK, we don't use the Oxford comma before the final *and/or* unless it is to make the meaning of the sentence easier to follow. For example, in the first sentence below, the word *and* is repeated, making the sentence a little confusing. The Oxford comma in the second sentence makes the meaning clearer:

> I went to the bank, the supermarket and Marks and Spencer.
> I went to the bank, the supermarket, and Marks and Spencer.

What are the two meanings of these sentences?

> I love my dogs, Fred and Martha.
> I love my dogs, Fred, and Martha.

The use of the Oxford comma in the second sentence clarifies that your dogs are not called Fred and Martha.

THE IMPORTANCE OF CHECKING YOUR WORK

There's no point in learning about grammar and punctuation unless you allow time to check your work when you've finished writing. If necessary, you might have to write less in order to free time to proofread. This is a good way to gain more marks for accuracy.

This is an unusual paragraph. I'm curious. How quickly can you find out what's so unusual about it? It looks so plain that you would think nothing was wrong with it. In fact, nothing is wrong with it! It is unusual, though. Study it. Think about it. You may still not find anything odd. But if you work at it, you might find out...

Have you managed to solve the riddle? The answer's at the bottom of the page.

REVISION: INDENTING AND BLOCKING

A paragraph is a section of a piece of writing that deals with a particular theme. There are two ways of showing that you have begun a new paragraph:

1. Indented Paragraphs

Indented Paragraphs look like this:

> This is the story of what a Woman's patience can endure, and what a Man's resolution can achieve.
>
> If the machinery of the Law could be depended on to fathom every case of suspicion, and to conduct every process of inquiry, with moderate assistance only from the lubricating influences of oil of gold, the events which fill these pages might have claimed their share of the public attention in a Court of Justice.
>
> But the Law is still, in certain inevitable cases, the pre-engaged servant of the long purse; and the story is left to be told, for the first time, in this place. As the Judge might once have heard it, so the Reader shall hear it now.
>
> —*The Woman in White*, Wilkie Collins

In the above example, it looks a little odd to indent the first paragraph of the chapter—this is a feature of older writing. With modern fiction and non-fiction writing, fewer people indent the first paragraph. After all, it's obvious that it's a new paragraph because it's the first one!

Blocked Paragraphs

Blocked paragraphs, on the other hand, have a blank line between them. They look like this:

> This is the story of what a Woman's patience can endure, and what a Man's resolution can achieve.
>
> If the machinery of the Law could be depended on to fathom every case of suspicion, and to conduct every process of inquiry, with moderate assistance only from the lubricating influences of oil of gold, the events which fill these pages might have claimed their share of the public attention in a Court of Justice.
>
> But the Law is still, in certain inevitable cases, the pre-engaged servant of the long purse; and the story is left to be told, for the first time, in this place. As the Judge might once have heard it, so the Reader shall hear it now.

ANSWER TO RIDDLE: There is no letter -*e*.

Traditionally, handwritten paragraphs are indented and typed paragraphs are blocked because it's easier to press the 'enter' button twice than to faff around with the indent tab.

There is no hard and fast rule, however. Many (but not all) publishers of newspapers, magazines and books indent paragraphs because this uses less paper and saves money. Some students today block handwritten paragraphs. The key point is that in a single piece of writing you either indent or block: never mix the two.

REVISION: PARAGRAPHING RULES

The famous *TipTop* rule is taught in many schools today. You need a new paragraph for a:

RULE	EXAMPLE
*TI*ME CHANGE:	Tomorrow...Later that day...At midnight...
*P*LACE CHANGE:	At school...At home...In the park...In the village...
*TO*PIC CHANGE:	Any new theme needs a new paragraph.
*P*ERSON CHANGE:	EITHER a new person
	OR a change of person speaking

Test Yourself!

The first sentence of a paragraph is called a topic sentence. It signposts a piece of writing and may contain one or more TIPTOP rule.

In this extract from *Alice's Adventures in Wonderland* by Lewis Carroll, everything has been deleted except the topic sentences. Label the reason for each new paragraph in the margin on the left, starting with the second paragraph. Is it a time change, place change, topic change, or person change? There might be more than one answer. Then check your answers on the next page.

Reason	
	Alice was beginning to get very tired of sitting by her sister on the bank, and of having nothing to do [...]
	So she was considering in her own mind (as well as she could, for the hot day made her feel very sleepy and stupid), whether the pleasure of making a daisy-chain would be worth the trouble of getting up and picking the daisies, when suddenly a White Rabbit with pink eyes ran close by her.
	There was nothing so VERY remarkable in that; nor did Alice think it so VERY much out of the way to hear the Rabbit say to itself, 'Oh dear! Oh dear! I shall be late!'
	In another moment, down [the rabbit hole] went Alice after it, never once considering how in the world she was to get out again.
	The rabbit-hole went straight on like a tunnel for some way, and then dipped suddenly down, so suddenly that Alice had not a moment to think about stopping herself before she found herself falling down a very deep well.
	Either the well was very deep, or she fell very slowly, for she had plenty of time as she went down to look about her and to wonder what was going to happen next [....]
	'Well!' thought Alice to herself, 'after such a fall as this, I shall think nothing of tumbling down stairs!'

Reason	
	Alice was beginning to get very tired of sitting by her sister on the bank, and of having nothing to do [...]
Time change and/or new person. If you don't regard a talking rabbit as a person, you could say topic change instead.	So she was considering in her own mind (as well as she could, for the hot day made her feel very sleepy and stupid), whether the pleasure of making a daisy-chain would be worth the trouble of getting up and picking the daisies, when **suddenly** a **White Rabbit** with pink eyes ran close by her.
Topic change (her reaction)	**There was nothing so VERY remarkable in that; nor did Alice think it so VERY much out of the way to hear** the Rabbit say to itself, 'Oh dear! Oh dear! I shall be late!'
	In another moment, down [the rabbit hole] went Alice after it, never once considering how in the world she was to get out again.
Time change and place change	The rabbit-hole went straight on like a tunnel for some way, and **then** dipped suddenly down, so suddenly that Alice had not a moment to think about stopping herself before **she found herself falling down a very deep well**.
Time change and place change	Either the well was very deep, or she fell very slowly, **for she had plenty of time** as she went down to look about her and to wonder what was going to happen next [....]
Change of time and/or new topic	
New topic	'Well!' **thought Alice** to herself, 'after such a fall as this, I shall think nothing of tumbling down stairs!'

Fascinating Fact!

Like indention rules, paragraphing rules have evolved over time. In this extract from *The History of Tom Jones, a Foundling* by Henry Fielding Jones (1749), Fielding organises the conversation between two people into a single paragraph:

When they came to the cross-roads where the squire had stopt to take counsel, Jones stopt likewise, and turning to Partridge, asked his opinion which track they should pursue. "Ah, sir," answered Partridge, "I wish your honour would follow my advice." "Why should I not?" replied Jones; "for it is now indifferent to me whither I go, or what becomes of me." "My advice, then," said Partridge, "is, that you immediately face about and return home; for who that hath such a home to return to as your honour, would travel thus about the country like a vagabond?"

Some of Fielding's dialogue paragraphs are over a page long, so the reader has to concentrate hard to follow who says what. Fortunately, the development of the *new speaker, new paragraph* rule makes it easier for the reader to follow conversations in modern texts.

Common Mistake

Can you spot the common paragraphing error in the joke? Check your answer on the next page.

Hannah was passing a classroom when she saw her good friend Anna sitting alone with a strange expression on her face.

Fearing the worst, Hannah charged into the room and confronted her friend.

"Anna, what's happened?" Hannah asked.

"It's my boyfriend, Matt," Anna replied. "He's ditched me for my best friend!"

"Hey, wait a second!" said Hannah. "Aren't I your best friend?"

"Not anymore," Anna said with a happy smile. "She is!"

The rule is: *new speaker, new paragraph*, not *new speaker, new line*. Many students write perfect paragraphs but, when it comes to speech, they begin a new line instead of a new paragraph.

If you usually indent paragraphs, your answer should look like this:

> Hannah was passing a classroom when she saw her good friend Anna sitting alone with a strange expression on her face.
>
> > Fearing the worst, Hannah charged into the room and confronted her friend.
> > "Anna, what's happened?" Hannah asked.
> > "It's my boyfriend, Matt," Anna replied. "He's ditched me for my best friend!"
> > "Hey, wait a second!" said Hannah. "Aren't I your best friend?"
> > "Not anymore," Anna said with a happy smile. "<u>She</u> is!"

If you usually block paragraphs, your answer should look like this:

> Hannah was passing a classroom when she saw her good friend Anna sitting alone with a strange expression on her face.
>
> Fearing the worst, Hannah charged into the room and confronted her friend.
>
> "Anna, what's happened?" Hannah asked.
>
> "It's my boyfriend, Matt," Anna replied. "He's ditched me for my best friend!"
>
> "Hey, wait a second!" said Hannah. "Aren't I your best friend?"
>
> "Not anymore," Anna said with a happy smile. "<u>She</u> is!"

STRUCTURING A NEW PARAGRAPH

As we have seen, a topic sentence introduces the theme of a paragraph. The rest of the paragraph then develops the theme. For example: in *The Count of Monte Cristo* by Alexandre Dumas, a young man called Franz faints after he witnesses an execution.

The theme of the topic sentence is what Franz notices when he recovers from his faint. The rest of the paragraph develops the idea of what he sees and hears.

Key
Pallor: unhealthy pale skin
Assuming: putting on
Masquerade costume: fancy dress, worn as a disguise at a carnival or party
Monte Citorio: a palace in Rome
Decease: death

> When Franz recovered his senses, he saw Albert drinking a glass of water, of which, to judge from his pallor, he stood in great need; and the count, who was assuming his masquerade costume. He glanced mechanically towards the square—the scene was wholly changed; scaffold, executioners, victims, all had disappeared; only the people remained, full of noise and excitement. The bell of Monte Citorio, which only sounds on the pope's decease and the opening of the Carnival, was ringing a joyous peal. "Well," asked he of the count, "what has, then, happened?"

You might be wondering why Franz's question to the Count is not in a new paragraph. This is because the paragraph is about Franz, and Franz is speaking. Therefore: *Same person, same paragraph!*

ADVANCED PARAGRAPHING SKILLS

In any piece of creative, descriptive, persuasive or explanatory writing, your teacher or the marker is looking for a range of sentence types. Deliberately varying the length of your paragraphs might also gain you extra marks. A simple sentence as a single paragraph, for example, stresses a point or emphasises a strong emotion.

In this extract from *The Yellow Wallpaper* by Charlotte Perkins Gilman, the narrator is suffering from a 'nervous depression'. Her husband is a doctor, and he has instructed her to stay in the bedroom of a house that they have rented for the summer. He orders her to rest, forbidding her to write in her diary. Defying him, she records her obsession with the colour and pattern of the wallpaper:

> *The front pattern DOES move—and no wonder! The woman behind shakes it!*
> *Sometimes I think there are a great many women behind, and sometimes only one, and she crawls around fast, and her crawling shakes it all over.*
> *Then in the very bright spots she keeps still, and in the very shady spots she just takes hold of the bars and shakes them hard.*
> *And she is all the time trying to climb through. But nobody could climb through that pattern—it strangles so; I think that is why it has so many heads.*
> *They get through, and then the pattern strangles them off and turns them upside down, and makes their eyes white!*
> *If those heads were covered or taken off it would not be half so bad.*
> *I think that woman gets out in the daytime!*
> *And I'll tell you why—privately—I've seen her!*

The short paragraphs become even shorter, as the narrator becomes more delusional. The author has superbly crafted paragraph lengths to deliberately emphasise the narrator's madness.

However, you don't want your reader to think that you're mad. Just have one or two short paragraphs in your written work; these will contrast with your longer paragraphs and prove that you can craft your writing.

Fascinating Fact!

Before paragraphs were even imagined, ancient classical Greek and Latin writing hardly had any spaces between words. Words were also written in alternating directions, which must have been confusing at times. Over time, scholars began to write from left to right, as we do today. Spaces to separate words developed, and punctuation at the end of sentences also became common.

The word *paragraph* comes from the Greek *paragraphos*. Early paragraphs, which divided sentences into groups, looked different to paragraphs that we recognise today. In the Middle Ages in England, scholars inserted the pilcrow (¶) or the hedera leaf (❧) between sentences to indicate a new paragraph.

Paragraphs in ancient manuscripts tended to be a line break and then an oversized capital letter of the first word in the next line. Sometimes, the capital letter was in the margin (outdenting). Visit the British Library website to see an example in the Old English manuscript of *Beowulf*!

In this extract from the children's classic *Peter Pan* by J.M. Barrie, the characters are flying in Neverland when 'fear' attacks them.

Use the modern pilcrow of two forward slashes (//) to show where each new paragraph should begin. Then, in the margin on the left, write the reason. Is it a time change, place change, topic change, person change or a combination? **One paragraph is a short sentence for emphasis.** The second paragraph has already been marked for you. Check your answers on the next page.

Reason	
	It [fear] came as the arrows went, leaving the island in gloom. **//** In the old days at home the Neverland had always begun to look a little dark and threatening by bedtime. [...] You even liked Nana to say that this was just the mantelpiece over here, and that the Neverland was all make-believe. Of course, the Neverland had been make-believe in those days, but it was real now, and there were no night-lights, and it was getting darker every moment, and where was Nana? They had been flying apart, but they huddled close to Peter now [...] "They don't want us to land," he explained. "Who are they?" Wendy whispered, shuddering. But he could not or would not say [...] Sometimes he poised himself in the air, listening intently, with his hand to his ear, and again he would stare down with eyes so bright that they seemed to bore two holes to earth.

DISCOURSE MARKERS

Discourse markers, sometimes known as connectives, are words and phrases that introduce paragraphs and sentences. They're useful because they add fluency to your ideas.

Below are some of the most common discourse markers. Read them and put them in the correct boxes. The first one has been done for you.

A and B: Giving examples and explaining ideas

for example   because   so   such as   therefore   consequently   for instance

Giving Examples	Explaining Ideas
for example	*because*

Reason	It [fear] came as the arrows went, leaving the island in gloom.
Time change and place change	**In the old days at home** the Neverland had always begun to look a little dark and threatening by bedtime. [...] You even liked Nana to say that this was just the mantelpiece over here, and that the Neverland was all make-believe.
Time change	Of course, the Neverland had been make-believe in those days, but **it was real now**, and there were no night-lights, and it was getting darker every moment, and where was Nana?
New topic (fear)/new time	They **had been flying apart**, but they **huddled close** to Peter **now** [...]
New speaker	"They don't want us to land," he explained.
Change of speaker	"Who are they?" Wendy whispered, shuddering.
Change of person. Short sentence emphasises his silence.	But **he** could not or would not say.
	Sometimes he poised himself in the air, listening intently, with his hand to his ear, and again he would stare down with eyes so bright that they seemed to bore two holes to earth.
Time & topic change	

Answers to Discourse Markers Exercise

A and B: Giving examples and explaining ideas

Giving Examples	Explaining Ideas
For example	*Because*
Such as	So
For instance	Therefore
	Consequently

Fascinating Fact!

Discourse markers add logic to your writing: they signpost your ideas. Without them, the connection between your ideas would be less obvious.

Test Yourself!

Continue to read the mixed-up discourse markers. Put them in the correct boxes.

C and D: Sequencing ideas and adding ideas

in addition   firstly   finally   next   what is more   also   moreover in conclusion   furthermore secondly

Sequencing Ideas	Adding Ideas
firstly	*in addition*

C and D: Sequencing ideas and adding ideas

Sequencing Ideas	Adding Ideas
firstly	in addition
finally	what is more
next	also
in conclusion	moreover
secondly	furthermore

Test Yourself!

E and F: Comparing and contrasting

likewise   however   in contrast   on the other hand   in the same way nevertheless   similarly   yet
as with   like

Comparing Similar Things	Introducing a Contrasting Point
likewise	however

G and H: Generalising, emphasising and introducing concluding points

on the whole   above all   as a result   indeed   therefore   generally   consequently   in particular
especially in general significantly so hence

Generalising	Emphasising	To Conclude a Point
on the whole	above all	as a result

E and F: Comparing and contrasting

Comparing Similar Things	Introducing a Contrasting Point
likewise	*however*
in the same way	in contrast
similarly	on the other hand
as with	nevertheless
like	yet

G and H: Generalising, emphasising and introducing concluding points

Generalising	Emphasising	To Conclude a Point
on the whole	above all	as a result
generally	indeed	therefore
in general	in particular	consequently
	especially	so
	significantly	hence

PUNCTUATION REMINDER

Some of the above discourse markers are easy to use: simply put them at the beginning of a sentence, add a comma and finish your sentence. For example: **On the whole,** *I love grammar.*

Other discourse markers are transition words called conjunctive adverbs (see chapter 14), so you might need a semicolon. A reminder:

> I like spelling**; however,** I prefer punctuation.
> I like spelling. However, I prefer punctuation.
> I like spelling. I, however, prefer punctuation.
> I like spelling. I prefer punctuation, however.

Highlight any conjunctive adverbs in the exercises above and aim to use them with the semicolon.

Common Mistake

What's wrong with these sentences?
  - However, in contrast, the poet suggests that life is to be celebrated.
  - In other words, alternatively, this symbolises society.

Answer

Both sentences begin with two sets of discourse markers that mean the same thing. Just one discourse marker is needed.

WHAT NEXT?

Can you guess the topic of the next chapter?

Joke Break
Don't spell incorrectly incorrectly, and spell incorrectly correctly.

Chapter 21: Homophones, Spelling Rules and Common Mistakes

It was Halloween, and some teenagers were walking home from a party. It was well past midnight so, knowing they'd be in trouble with their parents, they decided to take a short-cut through a graveyard.

Suddenly, they were startled by a tapping noise from the dark shadows of a tombstone.

Huddled together with fright, they cautiously advanced towards the sound.

To their relief, it was just an old man with a hammer and chisel, chipping away at one of the headstones.

"Oh!" cried one of the teenagers. "You scared us to death! We thought you were a ghost! What are you doing here so late at night?"

"Idiots!" the old man grumbled. "They misspelt my name."

Spelling is a grave subject.

WHAT ARE HOMOPHONES?

Homophones are words that sound the same but have different meanings. For example, *there, their* and *they're.* Let's see how much you already know.

Test Yourself!

Here are some commonly confused homophones. Read each sentence carefully and write the correct answers in the spaces. Check your answers on the next page.

1. They took _____ suitcases. _____ over ____! (there, their, they're)

2. Come _____! I can't _____ you! (hear, here)

3. I don't want _____ walk twenty miles. It's _____much! (too, to)

4. I _____ that _____ book yesterday. (read, red)

5. I _____a ball and it went straight _____ a window! (through, threw)

6. I'm _____ with this _____ game! (bored, board)

7. I don't care _____ the _____ is good or not! (weather, whether)

8. The disaster _____ed me badly. (effect/affect)

9. _____bus should be here in two minutes. (are/our)

10. I _____d Zara to go home and rest. (advise/advice)

Fascinating Fact!

Some words look the same but sound completely different. Did you know that there are at least seven different ways to say –*ough*? Try reading this aloud:

Even though rough people plough through my borough, I have a cough...and hiccoughs.

1. They took <u>their</u> suitcases. <u>They're </u>over <u>there</u>!
2. Come <u>here</u>! I can't <u>hear</u> you!
3. I don't want <u>to</u> walk twenty miles. It's <u>too</u> much!
4. I <u>read</u> that <u>red</u> book yesterday.
5. I <u>threw</u> a ball and it went straight <u>through</u> a window!
6. I'm <u>bored</u> with this <u>board</u> game!
7. I don't care <u>whether</u> the <u>weather</u> is good or not!
8. The disaster <u>affected</u> me badly.
9. <u>Our</u> bus should be here in two minutes.
10. I <u>advised</u> Zara to go home and rest.

COMMONLY CONFUSED HOMOPHONES

Some homophones are more commonly confused than others, so it's worth summarising the differences between them:

*   To accept (verb, meaning *to receive something* or *to agree with something*); except (means *not including*)
*   To advise (verb); some advice (noun)
*   To devise (verb); a device (noun)
*   To practise (verb); a practice (noun) *Notice a pattern?*
*   To affect (verb); an effect (noun). *Remember RAVEN?*
*   Are (verb: *We are* or *they are*); our (pronoun: Our mobiles are at home)
*   Here (opposite of *there*); hear (with your *ear*)
*   There (the opposite of *here*); they're (short for *they are*); their (to show possession: *their pens, their bags*, etc.)
*   Where (a question word), were (verb, past of *are*); wear (verb, *to wear clothes*)
*   Passed (an action: *He passed her the book*); past (to do with time: It's *long past your bedtime.*)
*   To (preposition, meaning *in the direction of*: *He's going to the shops*); to (part of an infinitive verb: *to walk, to talk, to eat*); too (means *also*: *I'm going there too*); too (means *excessively*: *You've given me too much food!*)
*   Through (preposition meaning *to go from one side to another*: *The train went through the tunnel*); though (means *however*); thorough (means *careful and detailed*: *His preparation for the exam was thorough*); thought (verb, past of *think*)

Test Yourself—Beat the Spellchecker!

Did you know that the spellchecker on your computer often misses spelling mistakes with homophones? This extract contains 27 errors that the spellchecker has missed. How many can you find? Underline them and check your answers on the next page.

Last knight, eye maid my weakly visit to my ant. I could sea that she had died her hare sew I said it looked grate. She lives inn a too-story house. She gave me a tore off her garden. When I past though, I eight a bury and a pair. They where affective. Aisle now brake this tail of and bee gone.

Last night, I made my weekly visit to my aunt. I could see that she had dyed her hair so I said it looked great. She lives in a two-storey house. She gave me a tour of her garden. When I passed through, I ate a berry and a pear. They were effective. I'll now break this tale off and be gone.

Joke Break	
Question:	What do you say to a sobbing English teacher?
Answer:	There, their, they're.

USEFUL SPELLING RULES

Words with -q

With English words, the letter –q is always followed by a –u. For example: *equip, frequent, queue.*

However, this rule does not apply to words from other languages. Examples include:

Qi	A Chinese word for a circulating life force.
Qin	A Chinese musical instrument.
Qiblah	The point toward which Muslims turn to pray.

These are useful words to know because you're broadening your vocabulary and knowledge of other cultures. These words are also worth a lot of points in Scrabble.

-I before -E except after -C

Joke Break
-I before *-E*
Except when your weird scientific neighbour with a conscience seizes eight weights.

The *-I before –E* rule is famous for its many exceptions. There are two full versions of the above rhyme, however. The first is:

-I before -E,
Except after -C,
Or when sounded as A,
As in *neighbour* and *weigh.*

This would explain the exceptions with the words *neighbour, eight* and *weights* in the introductory joke break. The second version of this rhyme is:

-I before -E
Except after -C
When the sound is EE.

This particular rule would explain the exceptions with *scientific* and *conscience* because the *-ie* sound in those words doesn't sound like an *-ee.*

The chart below is incomplete. Read the words and write them in the correct column. You should have five words per column in total. Check your answers on the next page.

believe, deceit, deceive, efficient, height, neigh, niece, piece, receipt, receive, reign, science, surveillance, their, thief, weight

Follows –I before –E rule because...	Doesn't follow –I before –E rule because...		
Has an EE sound	*Has -C followed by EE sound*	*Doesn't have EE sound*	*Has an A sound*
achieve	ceiling	ancient	beige

Fascinating Fact!

In England, the Bible used to be in Latin so that the church could control information: knowledge was, and still is, power.

In the sixteenth century, William Tyndale translated the Bible into English because many people wanted to read it in their own language. As this was illegal, his Bible was printed abroad by people who spoke no English. Subsequently, Bible readers copied the spelling mistakes. If copies of Tyndale's Bible came into their hands, English bishops burnt them. This resulted in more Bibles being printed abroad and, as they were already modelled on copies with poor spelling, the spelling in the reprinted Bibles became even more varied.

In 1539, three years after Tyndale was caught, hanged and burnt at the stake, Henry VIII's *Great Bible*, was printed. This was the first authorised Bible in English. Owning one of the Tyndale Bibles was still a risky business, however, so printers changed the spelling of words even more, hoping that no one would recognise an illegal Bible. Consequently, spelling patterns in words began to disappear. More people were learning how to read from the Bible and, by the second half of the 16th century, English spelling had become chaotic, with hardly anyone knowing any rules. In fact, some manuscripts contained different spellings of the same word.

Realising how bad the situation was, teachers came to the rescue!

To be continued...

Follows –I before –E rule because...	Doesn't follow –I before –E rule because...		
Has an EE sound	*Has -C followed by EE sound*	*Doesn't have EE sound*	*Has an A sound*
achieve	*ceiling*	*ancient*	*beige*
believe	deceit	efficient	neigh
niece	deceive	height	reign
piece	receipt	science	surveillance
thief	receive	their	weight

Exceptions to the -I before -E rule

Exceptions to the *I- before -E except after -C* rule include: *atheism, caffeine, protein, seize, weird.*

At the end of the day, English has absorbed so many words from different languages that it's impossible to create hard and fast spelling rules. All we can do is look for patterns. I suspect that the *-I before -E* rule will be the source of many jokes for years to come.

Common Spelling Mistakes—Part 1

Introducing Andy—Part 1

This paragraph contains five common spelling mistakes and one vocabulary error. Read the extract, number and underline the mistakes. Then write the corrections in the space provided.

My best friend has a good sense of humor. I like jokes aswell. That's why we get on with eachother.

Infact, I learn him alot of jokes.

1.

2.

3.

4.

5.

6.

Check your answers on the next page.

Fascinating Fact!

To help pupils with their spelling, sixteenth-century teachers created and published spelling lists. One of these teachers was Edmond Coote, whose 1595 list entitled *The English Schoolemaister* was popular because he recommended one spelling per word.

He also cut letters in words. One of these is *hadde*, which he changed to *had.*

My best friend has a good sense of <u>humour</u> (1). I like jokes <u>as well</u> (2). That's why we get on with <u>each other</u> (3). <u>In fact</u> (4), I <u>teach</u> (5) him <u>a lot</u> (6) of jokes.

Explanations

1. *Humor* is American spelling. Americans drop the *-u* with words ending in *-our*.
2, 3, 4 & 6 Always two words.
5. A teacher *teaches* (gives knowledge) and a student *learns* (receives knowledge).

Fascinating Fact!

Despite the effort of sixteenth-century schoolmasters like Edmond Coote, many English words still had more than one spelling. There were four spellings, for example, of *there, there, thare* and *their*.

With the aim of creating some order out of the English language, Samuel Johnson in 1755 published one of the most famous dictionaries in English history. In the preface, he stated his purpose: 'there was perplexity to be disentangled, and confusion to be regulated'.

In total, there were 40,000 words listed in his dictionary, each with a detailed definition. It took Johnson and his six helpers eight painstaking years to compile the dictionary because he introduced a new idea of adding notes on how the words were used. This included quoting the word in a sentence from literature. He also decided to link alternative spellings to differences in meaning— hence all the spellings of homophones!

By the time he had finished his dictionary, Samuel Johnson realised that it was impossible to order language because it changes all the time. He recognised that all he could do was record the spelling and grammar of people in the middle of the eighteenth century.

Common Spelling Mistakes—Part 2

Introducing Andy—Part 2

Andy's continuation contains six more common spelling mistakes. Find, number and underline them. Then write the corrections in the space provided. Check your answers on the next page.

We both like going to the theater. We enjoy the dialogs with the actors' different pronounciation of words. Any way, it's all marvelous and we're going to enroll on an acting course.

1.

2.

3.

4.

5.

6.

We both like going to the <u>theatre</u> (1).   We enjoy the <u>dialogues</u> (2) with the actors' different <u>pronunciation</u> (3) of words. <u>Anyway</u> (4), it's all <u>marvellous</u> (5) and we're going to <u>enrol</u> (6) on an acting course.

Explanations
1. *Theater* is American spelling: Americans change *–re* endings to *–er*.
2. *Dialog* is American spelling: Americans change *–ogue* endings to *–og*.
3. There's a *nun* in 'proNUNciation' (and a *noun* in proNOUNce!).
4. *Any way* as two words means *any method*. For example: *You can decorate your bedroom any way that you want. Anyway* as one word is an adverb, meaning *in any case*. You use it to change the subject, (*Anyway, I must dash!*) or pick up from where you left off (*Anyway, what were you saying?*).
5. *Marvelous* is American spelling. Americans don't have double *–l* endings of words. *Marvel* (GB) → *marvellous. Marvel* (US) → *marvellous.*
6. However, some British English words that end in a single *–l* might have a double *–l* with American spelling.

Joke Break
This joke is dedicated to Samuel Johnson.
Question: What do you say to comfort an exhausted man who's been compiling a dictionary for eight years?
Answer: There, there, thare, their!

Common Spelling Mistakes—Part 3

Introducing Andy—Part 3

Let's see how our stage-struck narrator is getting on. Once more, there are six common spelling mistakes. Find, number and underline them, writing your corrections in the space provided. Check your answers on the next page.

The program of study looks really interesting and all together lasts for two weeks. I need to get organized of course and look in to the details. They don't accept any body although every body is applying.

1.

2.

3.

4.

5.

6.

The programme (1) of study looks really interesting and altogether (2) lasts for two weeks. I need to get organised (3) of course and look into (4) the details. They don't accept anybody (5) although everybody (6) is applying.

Explanations

1. *Program* is American spelling. We only use this spelling in British English when talking about computer programs.
2. *All together* means in a group. For example: *The bags are all together in a heap. Altogether* as one word means *completely (I'm altogether shattered)*; *in total (I have two hundred books on my e-reader altogether)* or *on the whole (Altogether, I'm pleased with this book)*.
3. *Organized* is American spelling: Americans have changed *–ise* endings to *–ize*.
4. The word *into* is a preposition, and it means moving *towards the inside of.* For example: *I went into a cave.* In the extract, we have a similar idea of going into something (details).
5. *Anybody* is a pronoun. For an example of when to use *any body*, see the next joke break.
6. Similarly, *everybody* is a pronoun, which means *everyone*.

Joke Break
A headless chicken can't find its head. On the ground, its head shouts, "Have you seen any body?"

Common Spelling Mistakes—Part 4

Introducing Andy—Part 4
Read the next instalment of Andy's exciting story. This time, there are just five spelling mistakes to spot, underline, number and correct. Check your answers on the next page.

I also need to practice my audition speech everyday. I'm playing an aging man. I hope I get thru it okay. One day, I maybe famous!

1.

2.

3.

4.

5.

Fascinating fact!
Spelling mistakes or not proofreading can ruin lives. There's a story of a man on an overseas business trip who sent this message to his wife:

Having a wonderful time. Wish you were her.

Joke Break
Question: Why did the witch go to evening classes?
Answer: To learn how to spell.

I also need to <u>practise</u> (1) my audition speech <u>every day</u> (2). I'm playing an <u>ageing</u> (3) man. I hope I get <u>through</u> (4) it okay. One day, I <u>may be</u> (5) famous!

Explanations

1. A reminder that the verb *to practise* has an *–s*. However, it's worth noting that the American spelling of both the verb and noun is *practice*.
2. Always two words.
3. *Aging* is American spelling. With all due credit, they follow the rules and drop the *–e* when adding *–ing*. However, the British spelling keeps the *–e* so that the 'j' sound is soft, and there is no confusion when reading the word.
4. *Thru* is informal American spelling. Generally, *through* is used.
5. *May be* means *might be. Maybe* means *perhaps* (*Maybe I'll go to Spain this summer, or maybe I'll go to France.*).

Fascinating Fact!

Samuel Johnson injected his personality into some of the definitions in his celebrated dictionary. Although he received criticism for this, modern researchers enjoy seeing how he brought the dictionary to life.

From his definition of *lexicographer* (a person who compiles dictionaries), you have the distinct impression that his work wasn't easy: **Lexicographer:** *a writer of dictionaries; a harmless drudge that busies himself in tracing the original and detailing the signification of words.*

Scottish people, meanwhile, were offended by his definition of *oats*: **Oats:** *a grain which in England is generally given to horses, but in Scotland supports the people.*

Fascinating Fact!

You might be wondering from the commonly mistaken spelling of British versus American English words why there are so many differences between British and American spelling.

It's because of a dictionary.

In the seventy years that followed the publication of Samuel Johnson's celebrated dictionary, many words could still be spelt two ways. It was acceptable both in the United Kingdom and in America, for example, to write *humor* and *humour*.

Then, across the Atlantic, one man aimed to establish a distinct set of spelling rules to set the United States of America apart from England.

In 1828, Noah Webster published a dictionary, which greatly influenced the standardisation of American spelling. How did he do it? He simply picked the spellings that he liked best!

We'll end this chapter with a useful tip. If you're struggling to spell a word in an exam, use a different word!

Chapter 22: Prefixes and Suffixes

> **I am a female.**
> **FE = iron**
> **MALE = man**
> **Therefore, I am an iron man.**

Knowing about prefixes and suffixes helps with spelling and with working out what a new word means. Let's review some common prefixes and suffixes, zooming in one the ones that people might misspell.

PREFIXES

The bit that you attach to the beginning of a word is called a prefix. Here are some examples of prefixes and their meanings. How many do you already know?

anti = against → antibiotic　　　　　*De = change or reverse → demotivate*
audi = hear → auditorium　　　　　　*dis = not → disagree*
Auto = self → autobiography　　　　 *Ex = previous → ex-boyfriend*
aqua/e = water → aqueduct　　　　　*un = not → unnecessary*
bio = life → biology　　　　　　　　*trans = across → transatlantic*

COMMONLY CONFUSED PREFIXES

Fore- is a Middle English word, which means *before* or *in front of*. For example: *foreground* (the area at the front of a picture or photo) and *forethought* (thinking carefully about something before it happens).

For- is an Old English prefix that creates the idea of banning, rejecting, neglecting or destroying. Example words include: *forbid* (to refuse to allow)*, forgive* (to stop feeling anger or resentment).

Test Yourself!

Read the sentences and add *fore-* or *for-* to each underlined word. Then check your answers on the next page.

1. Oh, no! I've _____ <u>gotten</u> your name!

2. The sky is black; this is a _____ <u>runner</u> of rain.

3. Of course they'll win! It's a _____ <u>gone</u> conclusion!

4. He _____ <u>gave</u> her for eating the last chocolate.

5. In literature, _____ <u>shadowing</u> is when the author gives hints of what's to come.

6. I have a bruise on my _____ <u>head</u>.

7. I'll _____ <u>go</u> the chocolate pudding and have coffee instead.

8. Oh, my love! Why do you _____ <u>sake</u> me?

9. _____ *<u>thought</u>* is the opposite of *afterthought*.

10. My _____ <u>arms</u> are looking tanned!

1. Oh, no! I've <u>forg</u>otten your name!
2. The sky is black; this is a <u>fore</u>runner of rain.
3. Of course they'll win! It's a <u>fore</u>gone conclusion!
4. He <u>forg</u>ave her for eating the last chocolate.
5. In literature, <u>fore</u>shadowing is when the author gives hints of what's to come.
6. I have a bruise on my <u>fore</u>head
7. I'll <u>forg</u>o the chocolate pudding and have coffee instead.
8. Oh, my love! Why do you <u>fors</u>ake me?
9. *Forethought* is the opposite of *afterthought*.
10. My <u>fore</u>arms are looking tanned!

SUFFIXES

We add suffixes to the end of root words to form nouns, verbs, adjectives or adverbs. For example: *stud<u>ent</u>, stud<u>y</u>, stud<u>ies</u>, stud<u>ied</u>, study<u>ing</u>, stud<u>ious</u>, stud<u>iously</u>.*

Test Yourself—Spelling Rules!

Study each example group of words and then finish the spelling rule in the last column. The first one has been done for you.

Example words	Spelling changes to...	Rule
install will	instalment wilful	Ends with -*ll*. Drop the final –*l* when <u>adding –*ment* or -*ful*.</u>
fancy mystery pretty ready story	fanciful mysterious prettier readily stories	If the word ends with consonant plus –*y*,_____ _____
boy storey valley	boy storeys valleys	If the word ends with vowel plus –*y*, _____ _____
discolour honour honour labour vigour	discoloration honorary honorific laborious vigorous	If the word ends with–*our*, _____ _____
colour favour flavour	colourful favourite flavourless	Keep –*our* when _____

Example words	Spelling changes to...	Rule
install will	instalment wilful	Ends with -ll. Drop the final -l when adding -ment or -ful.
fancy mystery pretty ready story	fanciful mysterious prettier readily stories	If the word ends with consonant plus -y, the -y changes to -i.
boy storey valley	boy storeys valleys	If the word ends with vowel plus -y, there is no change.
discolour honour honour labour vigour	discoloration honorary honorific laborious vigorous	If the word ends with -our, change the ending of the word to -or before adding suffixes, -ation, -ary, -ific, -ious and -ous.
colour favour flavour	colourful favourite flavourless	Keep -our when adding other suffixes.

Fascinating Fact!

What do a-, anti-, dis-, il-, im-, in-, ir-, non- and un- have in common? They all make words negative. Interestingly, some apparently negative prefixes <u>don't</u> make words negative—for example, *inhabitable* and *inflammable.*

Test Yourself!

Fill in the blanks, adding a suffix to the word in brackets. If necessary, consult the chart above.

1. Good artists are _____(skill).

2. It was a _____ (labour) job to climb the mountain in the cold rain.

3. King Henry VIII closed many _____ (abbey).

4. He never laughs at my jokes! He's incredibly _____(humour).

5. She has a _____(rigour) approach to life.

6. The next _____ (install) of the story will be out soon!

7. Your new girlfriend is very_____(glamour).

8. I don't like that boring painting because it's_____(colour).

1. Good artists are <u>skilful</u>.
2. It was a <u>laborious</u> job to climb the mountain in the cold rain.
3. King Henry VIII closed many <u>abbeys</u>.
4. He never laughs at my jokes! He's incredibly <u>humourless</u>.
5. She has a <u>rigorous</u> approach to life.
6. The <u>instalment</u> of the story will be out soon!
7. Your new girlfriend is very <u>glamorous</u>.
8. I don't like that boring painting because it's <u>colourless</u>.

Words that end with -able and –ible

Both -able and -ible mean able to be. For example, readable means able to be read, and audible means able to be heard. Although there are exceptions, a general spelling guideline is:

If the word makes sense by itself, it will probably end in –able. **Example:** accept → acceptable
If the word does not make sense by itself, it's more likely to end in –ible. **Example:** divis → divisible

These spelling rules apply to the root word (the main word before adding the suffix):

If the root word...	Rule	Example	Becomes
ends in –e	drop -e before adding –able	inflate	inflatable
ends in –e	Keep the -e if dropping it would change the pronunciation.	change trace	changeable traceable
ends in consonant, vowel, consonant	double the final consonant	regret	regrettable
ends in a -y	change to an –i	pity	pitiable
has two syllables or more and ends in –ate	drop the –ate	calculate	calculable

Test Yourself!

Write –able or –ible in the space provided. Be careful! First, you might have to change the root word.

1. Is that behaviour really accept_____?

2. Sometimes I feel as if I'm invis_____.

3. Yes, I think it's achieve_____.

4. That was an unforget_____ film.

5. I'm not sure about that green stuff. Is it ed_____?

6. Is there a demonstra_____ reason for this?

7. Oh, no! That's horr_____!

8. I do't think your point of view is justify_____.

9. It's a make_____ project, definitely!

10. Oh, look! The Incred_____ Hulk!

1. Is that behaviour really accept<u>able</u>?
2. Sometimes I feel as if I'm invis<u>ible</u>.
3. Yes, I think it's achiev<u>able</u>. (DROP THE –E)
4. That was an unforge<u>ttable</u> film. (DOUBLE THE –T)
5. I'm not sure about that green stuff. Is it ed<u>ible</u>?
6. Is there a demonstr<u>able</u> reason for this? (DROP –ATE)
7. Oh, no! That's horr<u>ible</u>!
8. I don't think your point of view is justif<u>iable</u>. (-Y CHANGES TO –I)
9. It's a mak<u>eable</u> project, definitely! (KEEP THE –E OR IT SOUNDS LIKE 'MACKABLE'!)
10. Oh, look! The Incred<u>ible</u> Hulk!

Test Yourself!

Words that end with -ance, -ancy, -ant and –ence, -ency, -ent

Study each example group of words and then finish the spelling rule in the last column. The first one has been done for you.

Example words	Changes to...	New Suffix	Rule
app<u>ly</u> ins<u>ure</u>	appliance insurance	–ance	-y changes to –I before adding this suffix
occu<u>py</u>	occupant	-ant	
signifi<u>c</u>ance ele<u>g</u>ance signifi<u>c</u>ant extrava<u>g</u>ant	significance elegance significant extravagant	–ance -ant	
dominate hesitate tolerate	dominance hesitancy tolerant	–ance -ancy -ant	
adhere adhere	adherence adherent	–ence -ent	
pre<u>s</u>ence emergence de<u>c</u>ency emergency re<u>c</u>ent intelli<u>g</u>ent	presence emergence decency emergency recent intelligent	–ence -ency -ent	

118

Example words	Changes to...	New Suffix	Rule
app**ly** ins**ure**	appliance insurance	–ance	-y changes to –i before adding this suffix drop the silent -e before adding this suffix
occup**y**	occupant	-ant	drop the –y before adding this suffix
signifi**c**ance ele**g**ance signifi**c**ant extrava**g**ant	significance elegance significant extravagant	–ance -ant	suffixes follow a hard 'k' or 'g' sound
dominate hesitate tolerate	dominance hesitancy tolerant	–ance -ancy -ant	drop the –ate before adding these suffixes
adhere adhere	adherence adherent	–ence -ent	drop the –e before adding these suffixes
pre**s**ence emer**g**ence de**c**ency emer**g**ency re**c**ent intelli**g**ent	presence emergence decency emergency recent intelligent	–ence -ency -ent	suffixes follow a soft 's' or 'j' sound

EXCEPTIONS to the above rules include *vengeance* and *perseverance*.

Test Yourself!

Fill the gaps with -a or -e. For example: *We're an intellig__e__nt class!*

1. Sorry, Sir! He's abs____nt today!

2. Her face is radi____nt with joy.

3. With persever____nce, you can succeed.

4. She spoke with urg____ncy in her voice.

5. I'm reli____nt on you for your help!

6. "Who, me?" he asked, wide-eyed with innoc____nce.

7. A congreg____nt is a member of a congregation in a church or synagogue.

8. She can speak! She's making sense! She's coher____nt!

9. Andy's appear____nce on stage was impressive.

10. Here's the job vac____ncy that I was telling you about.

1. Sorry, Sir! He's <u>absent</u> today!
2. Her face is <u>radiant</u> with joy.
3. With <u>perseverance</u>, you can succeed.
4. She spoke with <u>urgency</u> in her voice.
5. I'm <u>reliant</u> on you for your help!
6. "Who, me?" he asked, wide-eyed with <u>innocence</u>.
7. A <u>congregant</u> is a member of a congregation in a church or synagogue.
8. She can speak! She's making sense! She's <u>coherent</u>!
9. Andy's <u>appearance</u> on stage was impressive.
10. Here's the job <u>vacancy</u> that I was telling you about.

Fascinating Fact!

You can choose between *dependent* and *dependant* when it's a noun. For example: *I have two children, so they are my dependents/ dependants.*

However, you can only use *dependent* when it's an adjective. For example: *I am dependent on passing my GCSEs to start A levels or an apprenticeship.*

Fascinating Fact!

In America, Noah Webster was working extremely hard on his *American Dictionary of the English Language.* It contained 70,000 entries (Johnson's had 40,000). Moreover, Webster was the first person to include American vocabulary such as *skunk*. Demonstrating extraordinary levels of commitment to his job, he learnt 26 languages. Why? He wanted to know as much as possible about word origins. It's incredible what you can achieve when you put your mind to something.

Words ending in –ary, –ery and -ory

If you're not sure which of these endings to use, here are some very rough guidelines; be aware, however, that there are lots of exceptions to the rules.

–ary

- **If the main part of the word is NOT a recognisable English word**, then it will probably end in –ary. For example: <u>library</u>
- However, this isn't as easy to spot as you might think, because many words that we think are English come from other languages. These words, for example, have Latin roots: <u>commentary</u>, <u>dictionary</u>, <u>secondary</u>.

-ery

- **If the main part of the word is a recognisable English word,** then it will probably end in –ery. For example: *trick → trickery*
- **Words that end in -er** sometimes make words that end in –ery. For example: *potter → pottery*

-ory

- Words that end in -or sometimes make words that end in –ory. For example: *advisor → advisory*
- Words that end in -ion sometimes make words that end in –ory. For example: *direction → directory*

Fascinating Fact!

In 1857, just under thirty years after Noah Webster's famous dictionary was published in America, a group of intellectuals in London called the Philological Society decided that it was time for another English dictionary.

To begin with, they had a few setbacks with their editors, and they also had problems finding a publisher. In fact, it wasn't until 1879—twenty-two years later—that the Oxford University Press agreed to publish the dictionary when it was finished.

In the same year, the Philological Society employed James Murray as their new editor, and he spurred everyone into action. He and his large team of helpers dedicated themselves to producing the dictionary, one volume at a time. They were confident that it would only take ten years.

Five years later—when the first volume was published in 1884—it went up to the word *ant*.

Test Yourself!

Read the sentences below and insert –*ary*, –*ery* or -*ory* into the space. Check your answers on the next page.

1. I'm so proud of his extraordin_____ achievement.

2. I need an example to go in this categ_____.

3. Following his operation, he's making a good recov_____.

4. Would anyone like to come with me to the nurs_____?

5. The uncooperative prisoner was put in solit_____ confinement.

6. I don't like snob_____.

7. The student made satisfact_____ progress in geography.

8. The sun's too hot for me to sit in this conservat_____.

9. I'm expecting a deliv_____ of some food tomorrow.

10. The bak_____'s just down the road!

Fascinating Fact!

There are only four words in the English language that end with –*cion*:

> *cion:* plant cutting, used for grafting
> *scion:* (1) alternative spelling to 'cion' (2) a descendant or heir
> *coercion:* using force to cause something to happen
> *suspicion:* thinking that someone has done something

1. I'm so proud of his extraordin<u>ary</u> achievement.
2. I need an example to go in this cate<u>gory</u>.
3. Following his operation, he's making a good recov<u>ery</u>.
4. Would anyone like to come with me to the nurs<u>ery</u>?
5. The uncooperative prisoner was put in solit<u>ary</u> confinement.
6. I don't like snob<u>bery</u>. ('snob' has vowel + consonant + vowel, so double the final consonant)
7. The student made satisfac<u>tory</u> progress in geography.
8. The sun's too hot for me to sit in this conservat<u>ory</u>.
9. I'm expecting a deliv<u>ery</u> of some food tomorrow.
10. The bak<u>ery</u>'s just down the road!

Fascinating Fact!

James Murray advertised for volunteers to read specific books and to copy quotations onto slips of paper, showing how words were used. These would then become examples in the Oxford English Dictionary.

After several years, he discovered that one of his volunteers was a prisoner in Broadmoor Asylum for the Criminally Insane. W.C. Minor was an American surgeon and military officer, who had killed a man in London. A highly intelligent man, he had studied medicine at Yale University.

Murray actually visited Minor at Broadmoor Asylum where presumably he thanked him for his contributions.

Minor's mental and physical health deteriorated. In the end, he was transferred to a hospital in America so that his family could visit him more easily. He died in 1920.

Words ending in –sion and -tion

This is our final section about suffixes, and we're going to examine the rules for using *–sion* and *–tion*.

Use the suffix *–ion* with:
1. Words that end in *-ss*. For example: discuss → *discussion*
2. Words that end in *–mit*. For example: *admit* → *admission*
3. Words that end in *–l, -n,* or *–r*) For example: *expul* → *expulsion, ten* → *tension, ver* → *version*.
4. Finally, say the word *revision* out loud and stop at the *-s*. Hold that sound in your head. That sound is always followed by the suffix *-sion*.

Use the suffix *–tion* with:
1. Verbs that end in *–ate*. For example: *educate* → *education*.
2. Most consonants (except *-l, -n,* and *–r*). For example: *reception*.
3. Say the word *station* out loud and stop at the second *–t*, which sounds like 'sh'. This sound is always followed by *–tion*.

Joke Break
Bad spellers of the world, untie!

122

Read the sentences below and insert –*sion*, or –*tion* in the space provided, and check your answers.

1. I like ac_____ films best.

2. Yes, I've made my final deci_____.

3. I'm good at addition but my long divi_____ needs work.

4. His descrip_____ of characters is amazing!

5. Would you care to give a dona_____ towards a worthwhile charity?

6. It's interesting how you both have a different ver_____ of the same story!

7. The admis_____ fee is £10.

8. Can we work together to find a solu_____ to the problem?

9. I feel revul_____ if I'm asked to dissect a rat.

10. There are different theories about the crea_____ of this world.

Answers

1. I like ac<u>tion</u> films best.
2. Yes, I've made my final deci<u>sion</u>.
3. I'm good at addition but my long divi<u>sion</u> needs work.
4. His descrip<u>tion</u> of characters is amazing!
5. Would you care to give a dona<u>tion</u> towards a worthwhile charity?
6. It's interesting how you both have a different ver<u>sion</u> of the same story!
7. The admis<u>sion</u> fee is £10.
8. Can we work together to find a solu<u>tion</u> to the problem?
9. I feel revul<u>sion</u> if I'm asked to dissect a rat.
10. There are different theories about the crea<u>tion</u> of this world.

The -ious and –eous Suffixes

Many adjectives end in –*ious* or –*eous*. For example: *ambitious* and *gorgeous*. There are no spelling rules although there are more words ending in –*ious* than -*eous.*

Fascinating Fact!

In 1928, the final volume of Murray's dictionary was published—nearly fifty years after he had started work as editor and just over seventy years after the Philological Society had proposed it.

Entitled *A New English Dictionary on Historical Principles*, it came in ten volumes. In total, it had definitions for over 400,000 words and phrases—330,000 more than Webster's American English dictionary.

Sadly, Murray passed away in 1915, so he never lived to see the end of his life's work. His legacy is a dictionary—now called the *Oxford English Dictionary*—that enjoys the reputation as England's greatest authority on the English language. It continues to be regularly updated, and you can read it online.

After this exciting journey through the history of spelling, let's tie up some loose ends.

Chapter 23: Punctuation (I)

I like cooking my pets and friends.

Forgetting to use a comma can make you look like a psychopath.

You might be wondering why, after beginning this book with a chapter about punctuation, I've left it almost to the end of the book to continue. The answer is that you've been revising punctuation all along. Remember those commas separating clauses or phrases in a multi-clause sentence? Or the commas in lists? It's impossible to study grammar and ignore punctuation. Let's review what we know.

REVISION OF THE COMMA

Here are the main uses of the comma:

After interjections
Remember chapter 5? Great! Unless it's an exclamation, separate an interjection with a comma. Example: *Well, who wouldn't?*

To introduce extra information
1. Remember the relative pronouns in chapter 8? Use a comma to introduce extra information. Example: *I'm going to London, which isn't far.*
2. The extra information might also be in a drop-in clause. In this case, the commas are similar to brackets. Example: *Erin, who's going to the party, scored full marks in the maths exam.*

To separate items in a list
Remember the lists of adjectives that we revised in chapter 9? Use commas to separate items in a list; you can also use the comma with lists of nouns, verbs and adverbs.

In literature, commas in lists are a useful device to develop atmosphere or build character. This is a description of Ebenezer Scrooge in Charles Dickens's *A Christmas Carol:*

> *...a squeezing, wrenching, grasping, scraping, clutching, covetous, old sinner!*

The list builds momentum to promote Dickens's opinion of Scrooge, drawing the reader's attention to the final word. This sets the theme of sin, helping to prepare us for the later visitations of the ghosts, who force Scrooge to reflect on his sins and their consequences.

To mark off introductory words or phrases.
- Remember noun phrases in chapter 3? ('Fog on the Essex marshes, fog on the Kentish heights.')
- Verb phrases in chapter 6? (Hearing no reply, she assumed he was out.)
- Adjectival phrases in chapter 9? ((Exciting and action-packed, the film delighted the audience.)
- Prepositional phrases in chapter 10? (Without my phone, I'm lost.)
- Adverbs in chapter 11? (Suddenly, he left.)
- Adverbial phrases in chapter 11? (During the performance, I fell asleep.)

Use a comma to mark off introductory words and phrases.

Before a co-ordinating conjunction in a compound sentence

Remember FANBOYS conjunctions in chapter 14? Most of the time, we use a comma before one of these co-ordinating conjunctions in a compound sentence. Example: *I went to market, and I bought some apples.* If the subject matter is closely related, there's no need for a comma.

With sentences that start with subordinating conjunctions
Remember that list of subordinating conjunctions in chapter 15? Use a comma when a sentence begins with one. Example: *Although I'm not keen on Brussels sprouts, I did my best to eat them all.*

To divide clauses and phrases
Remember chapters 16 (multi-clause sentences) and 17 (compound-complex sentences)? Review these chapters if necessary to revise how commas separate clauses and phrases.

With transition words (conjunctive adverbs)
Remember those transition words (or conjunctive adverbs) in chapter 14? We looked at examples of how to use them with commas:

Suzie was supposed to be walking to school; however, she was still eating her breakfast.
Suzie was supposed to be walking to school. However, she was still eating her breakfast.
Suzie was supposed to be walking to school. She was, however, still eating her breakfast.
Suzie was supposed to be walking to school. She was still eating her breakfast, however.

OTHER USES OF THE COMMA

So, when else do we use the comma?

To separate the name of someone you're talking to (direct address)
Note how the comma is used in the examples below:

We're going to learn to cut and paste, Jane!
Jane, we're going to learn to cut and paste!
We're going to learn, Jane, to cut and paste!

Joke Break
We're going to learn to cut and paste Jane!

With numbers higher than 999

Fascinating Fact!
The moon is 384,400 kilometres away from Earth.

With speech marks
The final use of the comma is with speech marks, which we'll examine soon. But first...

Put the commas in the correct places. Then check your answers on the next page.

1. This morning I woke up at seven leapt out of bed got dressed and brushed my teeth.

2. Fran pay attention!

3. Mount Everest is 8848 metres high.

4. I received an email which was mildly interesting.

5. Kieran who's in the same class as me is moving to Australia!

6. I think Molly that you're an excellent mathematician.

7. I may have seen them but I don't know where they are now.

8. Following our conversation I would like an apology.

9. The next day we all went home.

10. If however you change your mind let me know.

Fascinating Fact!

When the comma was invented more than 2,300 years ago, it looked completely different to the modern comma.

As we have already seen, scholars used to read aloud from texts, and silent reading was practically unheard of. A Greek scholar, critic and grammarian called Aristophanes of Byzantium invented commas in the 3rd century BC, so that people would know how long to breathe when they were reading out loud. He invented three dots:

- One for the top of a line
- One for the middle
- One for the bottom

Each dot showed the reader how much breath was needed to read the next part of the text, so its position was incredibly important.

In a short passage, a mid-level dot—called a *komma*—was used. It was a few hundred years before this evolved into the recognisable comma that we all know and love today.

The modern comma was invented by Aldus Manutius the Elder. Manutus was an Italian printer and publisher, who *invented the italic typeface.* Another credit to his name is that he developed the modern the appearance of the comma.

APOSTROPHE OF OMISSION

An apostrophe shows that at least one letter is missing when we omit (leave out) letters. This makes a contraction, a shortened word: *I'm (I am), you won't (you will not), they'll (they will or they shall).* Contractions can also show that numbers have been omitted from a date. For example: *'64 (1964).*

1. This morning, I woke up at seven, leapt out of bed, got dressed and brushed my teeth.
2. Fran, pay attention!
3. Mount Everest is 8,848 metres high.
4. I received an email, which was mildly interesting.
5. Kieran, who's in the same class as me, is moving to Australia!
6. I think, Molly, that you're an excellent mathematician.
7. I may have seen them, but I don't know where they are now.
8. Following our conversation, I would like an apology.
9. The next day, we all went home.
10. If, however, you change your mind, let me know.

Joke Break	
Pregnant woman:	You're! Can't! We're! Won't! It's!
Husband:	The baby's coming—your contractions have started!

Test Yourself!

How well do you understand how to use the apostrophe of omission? Shorten the words in the chart below, using an apostrophe to show where letters are missing.

Words in full	Contraction	Words in full	Contraction
I am	I'm	he would	
I have		he had	
he is		she will	
where is		she shall	
we are		it is	
we have		it has	
I am not		is not	
are not		let us	
cannot		must not	
could not		could have	
do not		could not have	
does not		shall not	
have not		will not	

Fascinating Fact!
Before you check your answers on the next page, did you know that *o'clock* is short for *of the clock?*

Words in full	Contraction	Words in full	Contraction
I am	I'm	he would	he'd
I have	I've	he had	he'd
he is	he's	she will	she'll
where is	where's	she shall	she'll
we are	we're	it is	it's
we have	we've	it has	it's
I am not	I'm not	is not	isn't
are not	aren't	let us	let's
cannot	can't	must not	mustn't
could not	couldn't	could have	could've
do not	don't	could not have	couldn't've
does not	doesn't	shall not	shan't
have not	haven't	will not	won't

Fascinating Facts!

1. We all know that to make a negative contraction we add *not* to a verb. For example: *he did not* contracts to *he didn't*. Did you know that we do this with all verbs except *I am not,* which contracts to *I'm not*?
2. Sometimes, you have a double contraction. It's used in very informal speech, and you need two apostrophes. For example: *could not have → couldn't've.* Nowadays, double contractions are incredibly rare.

IMPORTANT!

Never use the apostrophe of omission in a formal piece of writing: always write words out in full. (But you can use the apostrophe of omission inside speech marks.)

Fascinating Fact!

Double contractions used to be more common than they are today. In fact, some modern contractions have evolved from double contractions:

Original words	Old Contractions	Modern Contractions
shall not	sha'n't	shan't
woll not (alternative spelling for will not)	wo'n't	won't

So why did the first apostrophe in the old contractions disappear? The answer lies in the fact that apostrophes with contractions are used in informal writing. If you're writing quickly, you don't want to be faffing around with two apostrophes in one word. It's as simple as this: people couldn't be bothered to write two apostrophes, so they dropped the first one.

IMPORTANT! APOSTROPHES AND PLURAL WORDS

Never use an apostrophe to make a word plural. Every time you do this, a kitten dies.

THE APOSTROPHE OF POSSESSION

The second use of the apostrophe is to show possession or ownership. For example: *The **boy's** computer is on the table.* The apostrophe shows that it is the computer of the boy.

Singular nouns and irregular plural nouns

Add apostrophe before the *-s*. For example:

> the bag of the girl → the girl**'s** bag
> the toys of the children → the children**'s** toys

Regular plural nouns

Add apostrophe after the *-s*. For example:

> the staffroom of the teachers → the teacher**s'** staffroom.

What if the noun already ends in -s?

The above rules apply:

> The tiara of the **princess** (singular noun) → the princess's tiara
> The tiaras of the **princesses** (plural noun) → the princesses' tiaras

The same rules also apply when a person's name ends in *-s*: *The pupils of Mrs Lewis → Mrs Lewis's pupils.*

Test Yourself!

Read the phrases below and insert the apostrophe in the correct place. Check your answers on the next page.

1. The childs toy.
2. The boys toilets.
3. The books covers.
4. The mens names.
5. The three witches broomsticks.
6. The womans baby.
7. The womens babies.
8. Mr Joness office.
9. My mothers sisters boyfriend.
10. My mother-in-laws sons girlfriend.

Fascinating Fact!

A greengrocer's apostrophe is the name for an apostrophe that has been wrongly used to make a word plural (e.g. potato's, tomato's, carrot's). There go three more kittens.

1. The child's toy.
2. The boys' toilets.
3. The books' covers.
4. The men's names.
5. The three witches' broomsticks.
6. The woman's baby.
7. The women's babies.
8. Mr Jones's office.
9. My mother's sister's boyfriend.
10. My mother-in-law's son's girlfriend.

APOSTROPHE WITH IT'S AND ITS

It's with an apostrophe is short for *it is* or *it has.* When it is spelt without the apostrophe, *its* is the only word that does not use the apostrophe to show possession. For example:

> The cat drank its milk.
> The robot raised its arms.

APOSTROPHE WITH TIME AND QUANTITY

The apostrophe can also be used for time and quantity. For example:

> In the time of three days → in three days' time
> In the quantity of a metre of material → a metre's worth of material.

Joke Break	
Question:	Why are apostrophes difficult to date?
Answer:	They're too possessive.

Common Mistakes

Correct the errors in these real-life examples of apostrophe abuse. Then check your answers.

1. Its not mine, sorry!

2. Ladie's toilets.

3. On sale today: apple's, banana's and pear's!

4. Citizens Advice Bureau

5. I was born in the 1960's.

6. Is this your's?

7. Womens clothes

8. Hot soup's and coffee's

9. Saint Pauls Square

10. Some words contain lots of a's, i's and u's.

1. It's not mine, sorry!
2. Ladies' toilets.
3. On sale today: apples, bananas and pears! (There go three more kittens.)
4. Citizens' Advice Bureau
5. I was born in the 1960s.
6. Is this yours?
7. Women's clothes
8. Hot soups and coffees (Two more kittens.)
9. Saint Paul's Square
10. This is a rare exception, and the sentence is correct. You need to have the apostrophe to show that you are talking about plurals—otherwise, people might think you're writing *as, is* and *us*.

Fascinating Fact!

If a person's name ends in -*s*, you might sometimes see an apostrophe missing. For example: *Mrs Lewis' pupils*. This is an example of language changing over time, and it's a stylistic rather than a grammar-based decision.

Other people don't add apostrophe + -*s* to names from the Bible and the ancient world. For example: *Moses' stone tablets, Achilles' heel*. This is because adding an -*s* would change the pronunciation to *Mosesiz* and *Achillesiz*, which we wouldn't say. While the apostrophe shows possession, omitting the possessive -*s* retains the original pronunciation of the names.

BRACKETS (PARENTHESES)

Brackets (also called parentheses) contain extra information. If you delete them, your sentence will still make sense.

Joke Break
Anything in brackets can (not) be ignored.

Fascinating Fact!

Brackets can be traced back to the 14th century when scribes called them *virgulae convexae*, which translates as half-moons. Two hundred years later, they were being used to separate information in the same way as today. The use of brackets or parenthesis (Latin for 'insert beside') is explained by Richard Mulcaster, Elementarie in 1582:

Parenthesis is expressed by two half circles, which in writing enclose some perfit branch, as not mere impertinent, so not fullie concident to the sentence, which it breaketh, and in reading warneth us, that the words inclosed by them ar to be pronounced with a lower & quikker voice, then the words either before them or after them.

It's interesting to see the instruction about reading bracketed words in a lower and quicker voice—another reminder that most people in that historical period read aloud to others.

HYPHEN

A hyphen is a short punctuation mark (see examples, below). Traditionally, we don't leave a space before or after the hyphen. The only exception is when a hyphen is left hanging. For example: *I love **eighteenth-** and nineteenth-century literature.* A hyphen is used with:

1. Compound adjectives (see chapter 9). Examples: *a three-bedroom house, my eleven-year-old brother.* (**NB:** *a house with three bedrooms, my brother is eleven years old.)*
2. Some compound nouns (see chapter 3). Examples: *ice-cream, father-in-law* and also double-barrelled surnames, for example, *Mr and Mrs Worthing-Jones.*
3. Making meaning clearer. Example: *Twenty-odd teachers* are not the same as *twenty odd teachers*, who sound a little eccentric.
4. Nouns that begin with a stand-alone letter. Examples: *x-ray, t-shirt.*
5. Numbers: *twenty-one, twenty-two, twenty-three*, etc.
6. Some prefixes: *That's my ex-girlfriend.*
7. Prefixes attached to a word that must be capitalised. Examples: *anti-British, un-English.*
8. Hand-written essays when you reach the end of a line and realise that you haven't enough space to finish your word. Put a hyphen next to the incomplete word to show that you're going to split it and finish it on the next line.

Fascinating Fact!

Dionysius Thrax (170–90 BC), author of *Art of Grammar* is the first known person to use the hyphen in writing. The Greek grammarian used the hyphen to join two words, so they wouldn't be read separately.

In the Middle Ages, scribes used the hyphen to connect wrongly separated words. In the same historical period, the hyphen for a broken word across two lines was introduced.

When the Gutenberg printing press was invented in the 15th century, the individual letters of type needed to be held firmly in place in a frame. To secure the type, Gutenberg interrupted the letters in the last word of a line with a hyphen and carried the word over into the next line.

DASH

A dash is twice the width of a hyphen (—). Traditionally, there are no spaces before or after the dash. If you're typing, you can create a dash by pressing the hyphen button twice like this --. When you type the next word (remember, don't leave a space) and then hit the space bar, your two hyphens should change to the longer dash—just like this. So, when do we use the dash?

1. A dash is an informal—and quite dramatic—punctuation mark. You can use it in the same way as brackets, but the difference is that dashes emphasise the bit in the middle.
2. A dash is a lively punctuation mark, which shows a quick-thinking mind. Because of this, you can use it to indicate broken thought: *Yes, I really like that song—was that someone at the door?*
3. Or perhaps someone interrupts you—

Fascinating Fact!

General Sedgwick was a Union Army general in the American Civil War. He is famous for the irony of his last words: 'Don't worry, boys; they couldn't hit an elephant at this dist—.'

It's a truth universally acknowledged that Jane Austen, author of best-selling novels that include *Pride and Prejudice*, is known for her wit, her irony and her elegant writing style.

However, the late eighteenth- and early nineteenth-century author also used dashes in her writing to bring her characters to life. Mrs Bennet's excitement is almost delirious in this extract from *Pride and Prejudice*:

Jane's is nothing to it—nothing at all. I am so pleased—so happy. Such a charming man!—so handsome! so tall!—Oh, my dear Lizzy!

In 2010, Oxford University's Professor Kathryn Sutherland studied over a thousand pages of Austen's original manuscripts. The professor discovered that Jane Austen used capital letters and underlining to emphasise words, just as students do today in informal writing. She also used far more dashes than appeared in her novels. How did they disappear? William Gifford, who worked for her publisher, didn't like them, so he edited them out!

Joke Break
I wish I had the time for some punctuation jokes, but it's the end of the day—I must dash.

ELLIPSIS (plural: *ellipses*)

Modern ellipsis is a set of three dots. It has two uses:

1. To show that you're... trailing... off...hmm...I wonder what's for tea...
2. To show that words are missing, especially when you're quoting. In this extract from *Wuthering Heights* by Emily Bronte, the narrator wakes to find a ghost at his window.

Vocabulary Key:
Melancholy: sad
Discerned: slowly saw
Obscurely: in the darkness
Tenacious: clinging

...my fingers closed on the fingers of a little, ice-cold hand! The intense horror of nightmare came over me: I tried to draw back my arm, but the hand clung to it, and a most melancholy voice sobbed, 'Let me in - let me in!' [...] As it spoke, I discerned, obscurely, a child's face looking through the window. Terror made me cruel; and, finding it useless to attempt shaking the creature off, I pulled its wrist on to the broken pane, and rubbed it to and fro till the blood ran down and soaked the bedclothes: still it wailed, 'Let me in!' and maintained its tenacious grip, almost maddening me with fear.

You might have spotted that there's an ellipsis in square brackets. Editors do that to show that the original story is longer and they're leaving some of it out.

Let's imagine that you want to quote from the last sentence. At four-and-a-half lines, it's much too long, so we use ellipsis to show that you've omitted some words from the original text:

The narrator admits 'Terror made me cruel...I pulled its wrist on to the broken pane, and rubbed it to and fro till the blood ran down and soaked the bedclothes'.

The ellipsis replaces the unnecessary words in the middle of the original extract and makes the quotation crisper. Note that there's no ellipsis at the end of the quotation because I don't need it: I've finished my point. You only have ellipsis at the end of a sentence when you're traili...

Read the example sentences and insert brackets, an ellipsis, short hyphens or long dashes.

1. Hmmm___

2. Fifty___two people went to the party.

3. The holiday___ as usual___was fantastic!

4. My father___in___law is visiting at the weekend.

5. Yes, it was___ WHO did you say?

6. This writing is like a song___beautiful words, good rhythm of sentences and memorable.

7. The ghost 'wailed, "Let me in!"___ almost maddening me with fear'.*

8. It was definitely a never___to___be___forgotten moment.

9. Margaret Thatcher___Britain's first female Prime Minister___was a highly controversial politician.

10. All my school books___ including my favourite English book ___were eaten by the dog.

*Clue: Look for these words in the *Wuthering Heights* extract.

Fascinating Fact!

In 2015, Cambridge academic Doctor Anne Toner identified what she believes to be the earliest use of the ellipsis in English drama.

The ellipsis is in a 1588 edition of *Andria* by Roman dramatist Terence, translated into English. Interestingly, when the characters don't finish what they are saying, Terence uses three hyphens rather than three dots. The dots do, however, mark an ellipsis, i.e. left out words.

By the eighteenth century, people had begun to use more ellipses. These included a series of dots—but also hyphens or dashes—to show that words were missing from a sentence. Interestingly, many people used ellipsis to avoid being charged with libel (publishing something false about someone that damages their reputation).

---

1. Hmmm...
2. Fifty-two people went to the party.
3. The holiday (as usual) was fantastic!
4. My father-in-law is visiting at the weekend.
5. Yes, it was—WHO did you say?
6. This writing is like a song—beautiful words, good rhythm of sentences and memorable.
7. The ghost 'wailed, "Let me in!" ... almost maddening me with fear'.
8. It was definitely a never-to-be-forgotten moment.
9. Margaret Thatcher (Britain's first female Prime Minister) was a highly controversial politician.
10. All my school books—including my favourite English book—were eaten by the dog.

SPEECH MARKS

Speech marks are single or double inverted commas to show that someone is talking. In the examples, I'll use double inverted commas to avoid confusion with quotation marks.

Test Yourself!

Cover the rules in the right-hand column, and then read the example sentences. Work out the rules of how to punctuate speech. Check your answers by uncovering the rules.

	Examples	Rules
The speaker is first and the speech second:	She asked, "Would you like some dinner?" He replied, "Great, thanks!" She said, "Then you can take me to a restaurant."	a. Use a comma before the opening speech marks. b. The first letter inside the speech marks should be a capital letter. c. All other punctuation is inside the closing speech marks.
The speech is first and speaker last:	"That was a mean trick!" he exclaimed. "Sorry, couldn't resist it," she apologised. "Please don't do that again," he replied.	a. If an exclamation mark or a question mark are inside the speech marks, the pronoun that follows (unless it's the word *I*) is never capitalised. b. Use a comma or other punctuation marks before the closing speech marks.
The speaker splits the speech up:	"On second thoughts," he said, "let's go out!"	a. With the first half of the sentence, put a comma before the closing speech marks. b. Then introduce the second half of the sentence with a comma after the verb. c. Note that there's no capital letter with the second half of the sentence because it's continuing the same sentence.

When the same speaker talks for more than one paragraph

If the same speaker continues into a new paragraph, start each new paragraph with speech marks, but don't close the speech marks until the person finishes talking.

In this letter from *Pride and Prejudice*, the reader is reading a letter out loud:

> *"MY DEAR LIZZY,*
>
> *"I wish you joy. If you love Mr. Darcy half as well as I do my dear Wickham, you must be very happy. It is a great comfort to have you so rich, and when you have nothing else to do, I hope you will think of us. I am sure Wickham would like a place at court very much, and I do not think we shall have quite money enough to live upon without some help. Any place would do, of about three or four hundred a year; but however, do not speak to Mr. Darcy about it, if you had rather not.*
>
> *"Yours, etc."*

The person reading the letter is talking throughout—the speech marks at the start of each paragraph show this. At the end of the letter, the speech marks close to show the speaker has finished reading.

Use double quotation marks for the quote within a quote. For example: The politician said, 'Why did she call the man a "traitor"?'

Test Yourself!

Remind yourself of the rules for speech marks and then put the correct punctuation in the following sentences. Check your answers on the next page.

1. He said fancy going to London for the day?

2. Would you like to play rugby? she asked

3. The class said good morning, Mr Bruff!

4. Good morning, class! replied Mr Bruff

5. When she asked is the bus coming?

6. Let's call it a day he said

7. That book was brilliant! she exclaimed

8. When he saw his deadliest enemy, he said so...we meet again. Of all the places in the world, here you are.

    It's a year since you murdered my cat. She was my pride and joy. I'm still upset.

    Now it's time for my revenge.

9. I'd love she said another slice of that delicious cake...

10. When she asked is the bus coming? It's late!

Fascinating Fact!

In school, you will have been taught to use single inverted commas or quotation marks when quoting. However, you might have seen double inverted commas or speech marks around some quotations, especially on Twitter if you choose the *quote tweet* option. Why is this?

It's American English: Americans use double inverted commas to quote.

QUOTATION MARKS FOR QUOTING

Quotation marks are single inverted commas. The key points to remember are:

1. Unlike with speech marks, the full stop goes at the end of the sentence, after your quotation. For example: In *Wuthering Heights*, the narrator admits that the ghost of the girl was 'almost maddening me with fear'.
2. Grammatically, however, this example is not particularly good. It's better to pick the best bits and drop them into your sentence. For example: In *Wuthering Heights*, the narrator admits that the ghost of the girl was 'almost maddening' him 'with fear'.

1. He said, "Fancy going to London for the day?"
2. "Would you like to play rugby?" she asked.
3. The class said, "Good morning, Mr Bruff!"
4. "Good morning, class!" replied Mr Bruff.
5. "When," she asked, "is the bus coming?"
6. "Let's call it a day," he said.
7. "That book was brilliant!" she exclaimed.
8. When he saw his deadliest enemy, he said, "So...we meet again. Of all the places in the world, here you are.

    "It's a year since you murdered my cat. She was my pride and joy. I'm still upset.

    "Now it's time for my revenge."
9. "I'd love," she said, "another slice of that delicious cake..."
10. "When," she asked, "is the bus coming? It's late!"

OTHER USES OF QUOTATION MARKS

1. Put quotation marks around the title of poems, books and plays (when typing, you can choose to use *italics* instead). The quotation marks add clarity: Macbeth, for example, is a character in the play 'Macbeth'.
2. You can also use quotation marks when you're defining something. For example: In a dictionary, the letter *n.* after a word stands for 'noun'.
3. Quotation marks can show that you disagree with something. In this example, you might be feeling scorn: My 'best friend' let me down badly yesterday.

Common Mistakes

Read the sentences and correct the punctuation errors. Challenge: One sentence is correct. Which one?

1. WRITING ON A SIGN: "Don't walk on the grass!"

2. "You're going home!" He exclaimed.

3. Fresh 'eggs' for sale!

4. I grabbed my bag school bag and ran for the bus.

5. I'm blond however my brother has brown hair.

6. "I'm twenty one next month," She said.

7. I thought this work would be 'a piece of cake', but it wasn't.

8. Please "do not" park your car here!

9. She left the house but, remembering her phone was in her bedroom, returned home.

10. Victoria (who's terrified of snakes) touched one today.

Check your answers on the next page.

Joke Break
People who don't use full stops deserve a long sentence.

1. WRITING ON A SIGN: Don't walk on the grass!
2. "You're going home!" he exclaimed.
3. Fresh eggs for sale!
4. I grabbed my bag (school bag) and ran for the bus.
5. I'm blond. However, my brother has brown hair.
6. "I'm twenty-one next month," she said.
7. I thought this work would be a piece of cake, but it wasn't. (Clichés are bad enough—they don't need the extra attention.)
8. Please do not park your car here!
9. This sentence is correct because the middle part is a subordinate clause.
10. Victoria—who's terrified of snakes—touched one today. (The dashes emphasise her terror.)

ASTERISK

1. An asterisk is this symbol *. It's mainly used to point the reader in the direction of a footnote. For example, you might write an essay and, when you later check your work, you decide that you need to write another sentence. You don't have any space, so you use an asterisk. Your reader now knows to look at the bottom of the page for your word or phrase*.

2. Some people use three asterisks when writing a story:

***

The next section of the story contains a significant change of time or place.

Fascinating Fact!

The word asterisk comes from the ancient Greek word *asteriskos*, which means *little star*. It was known to be used two thousand years ago by Aristarchus of Samothrace, a Greek grammarian and librarian of the library of Alexandria. He used it when he was proofreading some poetry written by Homer.

COLON

It's interesting to see how punctuation can completely change the meaning of a sentence:

Joke Break
A teacher once asked her class to punctuate the following sentence:

A woman without her man is nothing.

The boys wrote: A woman, without her man, is nothing.
The girls wrote: A woman: without her, man is nothing.

1. So, when do we use the colon? In chapter 14, we examined how the colon can join two independent clauses. It works like a fanfare, announcing that the second clause is developing the idea of the first clause. For example: *I have something to say: you're fired!*

2. You can also use a colon to introduce a quotation: 'Two speech marks "walk" into a school.'

---

* This is a meaningless footnote. No-one ever reads footnotes, so there's no point in writing anything interesting.

3. The third use of a colon is to introduce items in a list. For example:

Qualities of a successful person include the following: imagination, a vision, perseverance and learning from mistakes.

SEMICOLON

Fascinating fact!

In chapter 23, we read about the Italian printer Aldus Manutius the Elder, who invented the *italic typeface* and the modern the appearance of the comma. He also believed that, at certain points in texts, you needed a punctuation mark to show a longer pause when reading out loud. This is where it becomes exciting: he invented the semicolon, which made its debut appearance in 1494!

1. In chapter 14, we examined how the semicolon is used with transition words, or conjunctive adverbs, seen in the example:

I like spelling**; however,** I prefer punctuation.

2. Semicolons are used to divide clauses of equal importance:

They wanted to speak but could not; tears stood in their eyes.
They were renewed by love; the heart of each held infinite sources of life for the heart of the other.
—*Crime and Punishment*, Fyodor Dostoevsky

3. A semicolon divides clauses or phrases in a long sentence, separating them into more easily understandable chunks. For example:

MR. UTTERSON the lawyer was a man of a rugged countenance, that was never lighted by a smile; cold, scanty and embarrassed in discourse; backward in sentiment; lean, long, dusty, dreary, and yet somehow lovable. At friendly meetings, and when the wine was to his taste, something eminently human beaconed from his eye; something indeed which never found its way into his talk, but which spoke not only in these silent symbols of the after-dinner face, but more often and loudly in the acts of his life.
He was austere with himself; drank gin when he was alone, to mortify a taste for vintages; and though he enjoyed the theatre, had not crossed the doors of one for twenty years. But he had an approved tolerance for others; sometimes wondering, almost with envy, at the high pressure of spirits involved in their misdeeds; and in any extremity inclined to help rather than to reprove.
—*Dr Jekyll and Mr Hyde*, Robert Louis Stevenson

In the extract below, find the subordinate clause or phrase and replace the commas with semicolons. WARNING: a clause or phrase contains a single idea, so you might need to leave some of those commas in! Check your answers on the next page.

I did a lot of things on Saturday, including the following: getting up at the crack of dawn, well, it felt like it, to drop my wife off at the airport, as she was going on a business trip, doing a grocery shop on the way home (the supermarket had just opened, and it was too good an opportunity to miss), taking my son, who's eleven years old, to a party, cleaning our house, which hadn't been tackled for nearly two weeks, so it was becoming a bit of an embarrassment, collecting my son, and, finally, enjoying a game of football on television with the rest of the family.

Fascinating Fact!

Some subordinate clauses don't need to be introduced by a colon because it would get in the way. This sentence sounds better without the colon:

The main points in an exam are to read the question carefully; to underline the key words; to spend at least five minutes—sometimes more—planning your answer; and to allow time at the end to check your work.

Fascinating Fact!

The first English printer to bring the printing press to England was William Caxton. In 1473, twenty-two years before Gutenberg's Bible was printed and fifty-three years before Tyndale's *New Testament* was published, Caxton printed the first book in the English language: *Recuyell of the Historyes of Troye*. This was quickly followed by other books, including Chaucer's *The Canterbury Tales*.

Caxton used just three punctuation marks: a forward slash (/) to show a group of words, a colon for a long pause and a full stop for a short pause. Here's an example and modern translation:

The thyrde temptation that the deuyl maketh to them that deye. Is by Impacyence: that is ayenste charyte/ For by charyte ben holden to loue god above alle thynges.

The third temptation that the Devil makes to them that die. Is by Impatience: that is against charity/ For by charity be holden to love God above all things.

You can see that using a full stop both for a short pause and to mark the end of a sentence makes this rather confusing to read. Unsurprisingly, English printers stopped using full stops for pauses about a hundred years later. They also replaced the forward slash with Aldus Manutius's more modern comma—and began to use the semicolon.

Joke Break
Proofread you're work if you want to be taken seriously.

I did a lot of things on Saturday, including the following: getting up at the crack of dawn, well, it felt like it, to drop my wife off at the airport, as she was going on a business trip; doing a grocery shop on the way home (the supermarket had just opened, and it was too good an opportunity to miss); taking my son, who's eleven years old, to a party; cleaning our house, which hadn't been tackled for nearly two weeks, so it was becoming a bit of an embarrassment; collecting my son; and, finally, enjoying a game of football on television with the rest of the family.

When you've finished checking your answers, read the passage out loud. Take a short pause at every comma and a longer pause at each semicolon. Can you hear the semicolons?

Test Yourself!

Put the colons and semicolons in the correct places. Check your answers at the bottom of the page.

1. I didn't do my homework instead, I watched a film.

2. It's coming towards us run!

3. He's cleaning I'm doing the shopping.

4. Clean the hall before returning the keys otherwise you'll lose your deposit.

5. Napoleon said 'History is the version of past events that people have decided to agree upon'.

6. I like cars she prefers motorbikes.

7. I have lots of things in my jewellery box necklaces, ear-rings, a ring and two watches.

8. In the summer holidays, I would like you to do the following clean and tidy one part of your bedroom every day, remembering the edges and corners, get some fresh air by playing outside play your music quietly because I'm writing a report and wash the dishes, all of them, when you've finished with them.

Answers

1. I didn't do my homework; instead, I watched a film.
2. It's coming towards us: run!
3. He's cleaning; I'm doing the shopping.
4. Clean the hall before returning the keys; otherwise, you'll lose your deposit.
5. Napoleon said: 'History is the version of past events that people have decided to agree upon'.
6. I like cars; she prefers motorbikes.
7. I have lots of things in my jewellery box: necklaces, ear-rings, a ring and two watches.
8. In the summer holidays, I would like you to do the following: clean and tidy one part of your bedroom every day, remembering the edges and corners; get some fresh air by playing outside; play your music quietly because I'm writing a report; and wash the dishes, all of them, when you've finished with them.

TO CONCLUDE

Well done! You've just finished reviewing all the punctuation marks! The final step of our journey is to use your knowledge of grammar to craft ideas.

Chapter 25: Rhetorical Devices

> ***Rhetoric is the art of ruling the minds of men.***
> —Plato

Rhetoric is the art of persuasive speaking or writing, using particular techniques to craft your ideas. As the ancient Greek philosopher Plato makes clear, you can achieve a lot through rhetoric. The ancient Greeks used to teach rhetoric alongside grammar and logic; in Western Europe, it was an essential part of education until the late nineteenth century. Shakespeare was also educated in grammar and rhetoric, which were highly esteemed in Elizabethan England as tools for moving people's feelings.

Many of us speak or write to express a point of view. This might be to inform, explain, describe, argue a point or persuade. Effective speaking and writing is crafted to appeal to particular audiences. In this chapter, we'll review basic rhetorical devices that will help to make your spoken and written ideas more convincing. These are also useful life skills.

You might be familiar with the acronyms AFOREST, DAFOREST or ARRESTED, which are good for memorising rhetorical devices. These acronyms were used successfully by many students across the country until, in June 2017, an examiner report stated that the examiners are no longer interested in fake anecdotes, statistics, surveys or expert opinions because they're not convincing. There are plenty of rhetorical devices that we can still use, however.

Fascinating Fact!

Three of the most famous ancient Greek orators and philosophers include:

- Socrates (469-399 BC): he called oration *flattery* and was more interested in philosophy. Nevertheless, he developed a questioning process which aimed to develop insight and understanding of particular issues.
- Plato (427-347 BC): A student of Socrates, he was also a philosopher and a mathematician. He wrote dialogues of conversations between Socrates and himself, which were then used to teach a range of subjects, including rhetoric.
- Aristotle (400-320 BC): An extensive writer, philosopher and teacher, he developed systems to understand and teach rhetoric.

THE BASICS

This CREEP RRR acronym summarises rhetorical devices that can be used as a starting point in any speech or piece of writing to express a viewpoint:

Counterargument	**R**ule of Three
Rhetorical question	**R**epetition
Emotive language	**R**eflection
Exaggeration	
Pronouns	

Shakespeare's play *Julius Caesar* contains marvellous examples of the above, so I'm going to use examples from his play to illustrate these techniques. If you're interested in reading the full script with a line-by-line translation into modern English and an analysis of each scene, *Mr Bruff's Guide to 'Julius Caesar'* is available at www.mrbruff.com or in paperback on Amazon.

Counterargument

By acknowledging and dismissing the opposite view to yours, you're structuring your argument to make it more convincing.

Mark Antony does this in Shakespeare's *Julius Caesar* when, at Caesar's funeral, he argues against the assassin Brutus's claim that Caesar deserved to die because he was ambitious:

Original Play	Modern Translation
He hath brought many captives home to Rome, Whose ransoms did the general coffers fill: Did this in Caesar seem ambitious? When that the poor have cried, Caesar hath wept; Ambition should be made of sterner stuff: Yet Brutus says he was ambitious, And Brutus is an honourable man.	He brought many captives home to Rome, Whose ransoms brought wealth to our city: Did this make Caesar appear ambitious? When the poor cried, Caesar wept too; Someone who's ambitious should be made of sterner stuff: Yet Brutus says he was ambitious, And Brutus is an honourable man.

By acknowledging the accusations of ambition against Caesar and dismissing them with hard evidence, Mark Antony weakens Brutus's argument, hinting that Brutus is not honourable.

Rhetorical question.

Why do I need to write a question that my reader won't answer? You answer it yourself. This focuses the reader on your point. In this example, Mark Antony cleverly positions his rhetorical question:

Original Play	Modern Translation
I thrice presented him a kingly crown, Which he did thrice refuse. Was this ambition? Yet Brutus says he was ambitious, And sure he is an honourable man.	I presented him with a king's crown three times, And, three times he refused it. Was this ambition? Yet Brutus says he was ambitious, And I'm sure he [Brutus] is an honourable man.

Mark Antony sandwiches the rhetorical question between evidence of Caesar not being ambitious (refusing the crown three times) and Brutus's accusation of Caesar being ambitious. By answering his own rhetorical question, Mark Antony deliberately encourages the crowd to question Brutus's honour.

Fascinating Fact!
If you ask a rhetorical question and then answer it, this is called **hypophora** (pronounced hippo-FOR-uh).

Emotive language

This is deliberately choosing words to make your reader feel particular emotions. With a neutral statement, we don't feel anything. For example: *A student went to school.* Let's play with emotive words and change the reader's feelings:
- A prize-winning student walked confidently and cheerfully to school.
- A reluctant student dragged himself wearily to school.
- A sports scholar bounced energetically to school.
- A lonely Year 7 student, who had no friends, limped to school, dragging her heavy bag, hoping that the bullies wouldn't catch her.

Remember that you need to think carefully about your vocabulary and the effect that you want it to have on your audience.

Towards the end of *Julius Caesar*, Mark Antony loses his temper and confronts his enemies Brutus and Casca. Shakespeare uses emotive language to show Mark Antony's hatred towards the pair.

Original Play	Modern Translation
Villains! You did not so, when your vile daggers Hack'd one another in the sides of Caesar: You show'd your teeth like apes, and fawn'd like hounds, And bow'd like bondmen, kissing Caesar's feet; Whilst damned Casca, like a cur, behind Struck Caesar on the neck. O, you flatterers!	Villains! You didn't warn us when your vile daggers Hack'd each other in Caesar's sides: You smiled insincerely like apes, and fawned like dogs, And bowed like servants, kissing Caesar's feet; Whilst damned Casca, like a mongrel dog, from behind Struck Caesar on the neck. Oh, you flatterers!

Shakespeare crafts Mark Antony's emotive language in a range of ways:
- **Insults:** 'Villains!' and 'O you flatterers!'
- **Emotive adjective:** 'vile'.
- **Emotive verbs:** 'hack'd' and '[s]truck' to recreate the violence of the murder and illustrate the conspirators' bloodlust.
- **Animal imagery with similes:** 'show'd your teeth like apes, and fawn'd like hounds' to underline the hypocrisy of Brutus and Casca, who smiled like friends and pretended slavish, dog-like devotion while Casca stabbed Caesar in the back. The animal imagery also dehumanises the pair, adding to the insult.
- **Simile of servile behaviour:** 'bow'd like bondmen, kissing Caesar's feet'. This creates the visual symbolism of the pair publicly revering Caesar, openly acknowledging his higher status. The contrasting imagery of them doing this while Casca with the simile 'like a cur' (an unwanted, stray dog) creeps up 'behind' Caesar to kill him emphasises their duplicity and betrayal.

Exaggeration

Exaggeration is often used for emphasis or humour. In Act 1, Scene 1 of *Julius Caesar*, the government official Flavius is angry because the crowd is celebrating the returning Julius Caesar's victory—he has killed Pompey, whom the crowd previously loved. Flavius tells the crowd to go to the Tiber river and fill it with their tears. They should cry until their tears reach the top of the highest river banks:

Original Play	Modern Translation
Assemble all the poor men of your sort, Draw them to Tiber banks, and weep your tears Into the channel till the lowest stream Do kiss the most exalted shores of all.	Gather together all the poor men like yourselves, Lead them to the banks of the river Tiber and all of you weep your tears Into the river until even at the lowest ebb the river level Swells enough to reach the highest banks of all.

Flavius uses exaggeration to emphasise his anger and to communicate how sad the crowd should be feeling.

Fascinating Fact!
Another word for exaggeration is **hyperbole**, pronounced high-PURR-bull-ee.

Pronouns

Remember that your aim is to encourage your audience to agree with what you are saying or writing. By deliberately using pronouns such as *we, us,* or *you and I,* you are including your audience and hopefully winning more support. (Alternatively, you could use the contrasting pronouns *him, her* or *them* to distance your audience from people who hold alternative points of view.)

In Act 3, Scene 2 of *Julius Caesar*, Mark Antony includes his listeners, creating a rapport with them with the underlined pronouns.

Original Play	Modern Translation
O, what a fall was there, <u>my</u> countrymen! Then <u>I</u>, and <u>you</u>, and <u>all of us</u> fell down, Whilst bloody treason flourish'd over <u>us</u>. O, now <u>you</u> weep, and <u>I</u> perceive <u>you</u> feel The dint of pity. These are gracious drops. Kind souls, what weep <u>you</u> when <u>you</u> but behold <u>Our</u> Caesar's vesture wounded? Look <u>you</u> here, Here is himself, marr'd, as <u>you</u> see, with traitors.	Oh, what a fall it was, <u>my</u> countrymen! Then <u>I</u> and <u>you</u> and <u>all of us</u> fell down, Whilst bloody treason triumphed over <u>us.</u> Oh, now <u>you</u> are weeping, and <u>I</u> am aware that <u>you</u> feel The stroke of pity. These are compassionate tears. Kind souls, how <u>you</u> weep when <u>you</u> observe Merely <u>our</u> Caesar's wounded clothing? Look here, at this, Here is the man himself, mangled, as <u>you</u> see, by traitors.

Mark Antony manipulates the crowd with his use of inclusive pronouns, implying that the citizens were also betrayed.

Rule of three

The Rule of Three is a set of three words or ideas that make the point more memorable. The historical Julius Caesar is famous in 46 BC for having said (in Latin): 'I came, I saw, I conquered'.

If you can add alliteration (words that begin with the same sound) to your three words, this heightens their impact. In this extract from Act 3, Scene 2, Mark Antony in apparent humbleness tells the crowd that he is 'plain blunt man'. Then he uses the rule of three—twice.

Original Play	Modern Translation
For I have neither **wit**, nor **words**, nor **worth**, **Action**, nor **utterance**, nor the **power of speech** To stir men's blood	For I have neither **intellectual brilliance**, nor **fluency**, nor **weight of authority**, **Presence**, nor **delivery**, nor the **power of speech** To stir men to action

Through his use of the rule of three (and alliteration with the first example), we see that, despite professing to be a plain, blunt man, Mark Antony is a great orator and a sophisticated manipulator.

The repetition of 'nor', a coordinating conjunction, adds rhythm to his list, building momentum and passion. This is called **polysyndeton** (pronounced Polly-SIN-ditton).

Repetition

Mark Antony uses repetition at various points in his famous speech in Act 3, Scene 2. For example, he repeats 'Brutus says he was ambitious, /And Brutus is an honourable man' four times to openly flatter Brutus. As mentioned above, Mark Antony's evidence contradicts Brutus's point about Caesar's ambition, thereby weakening Brutus's argument. Antony also repeats Brutus's name to hammer home the connection between Brutus and Caesar's death, making sure the crowd knows whom to blame. We have a considerable amount of irony because, although on the surface Antony appears respect Caesar's murderers, his use of repetition encourages the crowd to question the honour of Brutus.

Mark Antony also uses repetition when he looks at the place where Caesar was murdered:

Original Play	Modern Translation
Here didst thou fall; and **here** thy hunters stand,	It is **here** that you fell; and it is **here** that your hunters are standing,

The repetition of 'here' implies that Antony is marking the spot, fixing in his heart the place that Caesar was murdered—for his later revenge.

Reflection

A reflection is a serious thought or consideration. Mark Antony shows Caesar's blooded cloak to the crowd, creating a vivid visual aid. He employs the cloak to trigger an apparent reflection, appealing to shared knowledge:

Original Play	Modern Translation
You all do know this mantle. I remember	You all recognise this cloak. I remember
The first time ever Caesar put it on;	The first time ever that Caesar put it on;
'Twas on a summer's evening in his tent,	It was on a summer's evening in his tent,
That day he overcame the Nervii.	On the day he overcame the Nervii warriors.

By using the determiner 'that' with the noun 'day', Antonio is assuming that everyone knows when Caesar 'overcame the Nervii'. This would be the case, as it was a heroic day for Caesar who, in 57 BC, defeated the Nervians (or Nervii) in Northern France. His skill, determination and knowledge of tactics, coupled with the arrival of reinforcements, turned an apparently lost cause into a celebrated victory for the Romans. Through his use of reflection, Antony reminds the crowd that Julius Caesar was a war hero and charismatic leader of men, appealing to their sense of national pride and loyalty.

Fascinating Fact!
The art of rhetoric can be traced back to the fifth century BC. Between 466 and 465 BC, a violent and murderous tyrant called Thrasybulus of Syracuse executed or exiled people so that he could seize their property.
As a result, many of the dispossessed tried to recover their land through the law. Corax and his pupil Tisias helped them by founding rhetoric: they created a method of structuring speeches that could be used in court.
Fortunately, the unhappy citizens did not have to endure Thrasybulus for long: he ruled for just eleven months before he was overthrown by members of his own family.

Read each extract and in the right-hand column label one of the following rhetorical devices:

Counterargument   **R**ule of Three
Rhetorical question   **R**epetition
Emotive language   **R**eflection
Exaggeration
Pronouns

	Example	Rhetorical Device
1.	'SUPPOSING that Truth is a woman—**what then?**' *—Beyond Good and Evil,* Friedrich Nietzsche	
2.	'I found it hard to think evil of such a **dear, kind old** clergyman.' *—The Adventures of Sherlock Holmes,* Sir Arthur Conan Doyle	
3.	'O **Captain!** my **Captain! rise up** and hear the bells; **Rise up**—for you the flag is flung—for you the bugle trills...' *O Captain! My Captain!* Walt Whitman	
4.	'The world must be made safe for democracy. Its peace must be planted upon the tested foundations of political liberty. **We** have no selfish ends to serve. **We** desire no conquest, no dominion. **We** seek no indemnities for ourselves, no material compensation for the sacrifices **we** shall freely make. **We** are but one of the champions of the rights of mankind. **We** shall be satisfied when those rights have been made as secure as the faith and the freedom of nations can make them.' *–The World Must be made safe for Democracy,* Woodrow Wilson, 2nd April 1917.	
5.	'Fellow-citizens, above your national, tumultuous joy, **I hear the mournful wail of millions! whose chains, heavy and grievous yesterday**, are, to-day, rendered more intolerable by the jubilee shouts that reach them. [...] **To forget them, to pass lightly over their wrongs**, and to chime in with the popular theme, **would be treason most scandalous and shocking**, and would make me a reproach before God and the world. My subject, then, fellow-citizens, is American slavery.' *--The Meaning of the Fourth of July to a Negro,* Frederick Douglass (1852)	
6.	'**I know I have the body of a weak, feeble woman; but I have the heart and stomach of a king – and of a King of England too**, and think foul scorn that Parma or Spain, or any prince of Europe, should dare to invade the borders of my realm.' *--Before the failed invasion of the Spanish Armada,* Queen Elizabeth I (1588)	
7.	'**An hundred years should go to praise** Thine eyes and on thy forehead gaze; **Two hundred to adore** each breast; But **thirty thousand to the rest**.' *—To His Coy Mistress,* Andrew Marvell	
8.	'There was once a time when New England **groaned** under the actual pressure of **heavier wrongs** than those **threatened** ones which brought on the Revolution.' *—Twice-Told Tales* by Nathaniel Hawthorne	

Check your answers on the next page.

1. Rhetorical question
2. Rule of three
3. Repetition
4. Inclusive we
5. Reflection
6. Counterargument
7. Exaggeration (hyperbole)
8. Emotive language

Fascinating Fact!

Aristotle identified three persuasive methods that could be used in rhetoric: logos, ethos and pathos.

- **Logos** is an appeal to logic, using reason to persuade.
- **Ethos** is an appeal to ethics. The idea is to convince an audience that you are of good character and can be trusted.
- **Pathos** is an appeal to emotion, aiming to get an emotional response from an audience.

HOW TO STRUCTURE A GOOD SPEECH

Like Plato, the Roman orator Cicero believed that a good speech can make an audience believe anything. In around 50 BC, he wrote *Rhetorica ad Herennium*, which explained The Five Canons of Rhetoric. Each canon was a rule for judging a good speech:

1. **Invention:** researching, planning and developing ideas.
2. **Arrangement:** ordering and structuring ideas for impact.
3. **Style:** planning how to deliver ideas. Do you plan to instruct, move or please your audience? Which words will you use? Which sentence structures, figures of speech and other rhetorical devices will you use?
4. **Memory:** memorising your speech.
5. **Delivery:** rehearsing your speech, paying particular attention to voice and gestures.

Sadly, your ability to give an outstanding presentation isn't worth any marks at GCSE any more. This is a shame because it's an important life skill, greatly valued by employers.

However, two thousand years after they were written, we can still apply the first three canons to the planning of writing to express an opinion. It's important to stress that your ideas come first: only after you know what you are going to say do you select rhetorical devices to support your points.

Fascinating Fact!

Quintilian (35-100 AD) is another famous figure from ancient Greece. He opened a public school of rhetoric and wrote a textbook. In *Institutio Oratoria,* which was in twelve volumes, Quintilian developed Cicero's Five Canons of Rhetoric.

If you're interested in stretching and challenging yourself with more rhetorical devices, we'll examine some in the next chapter. In the meantime...

Joke Break
What do you get when you mix a joke with a rhetorical question?

> ***Speech is power: speech is to persuade, to convert, to compel.***
> —Ralph Waldo Emerson

This exciting bonus chapter aims to develop and extend your knowledge of rhetorical devices. A word of warning: don't aim to use all of them in a single piece of writing. If you do, your writing might sound contrived and unconvincing.

HUMOUR

If people laugh with you, they're more likely to agree with your point of view. We'll begin by reviewing different kinds of irony before moving on to satire and parody.

Verbal irony

Verbal irony is the difference between what you say and what you mean. It's very similar to sarcasm; however, with sarcasm you deliberately intend to hurt someone's feelings.

People sometimes use irony to emphasise a point or to create humour. A good example is the famous first sentence of Jane Austen's *Pride and Prejudice*:

> *It is a truth universally acknowledged, that a single man in possession of a good fortune, must be in want of a wife.*

When we read the first chapter, we learn the real meaning behind these words: single young ladies pressurised by anxious mothers are in want of a rich husband. The pompous *It is a truth universally acknowledged* adds to the humour.

> **Joke Break**
> ***Irony*** is when someone writes ***Your an idiot***.

Situational irony

To understand situational irony, you first need to look at context—the situation that the people are in. For example, in *The Rime of the Ancient Mariner* by Samuel Taylor Coleridge, the crew of a ship have run out of water:

> *Water, water, everywhere,*
> *And all the boards did shrink;*
> *Water, water, everywhere,*
> *Nor any drop to drink.*

The context is that they're surrounded by water—the sea—which they can't drink. This makes the situation—dying of thirst—ironic.

Dramatic irony

With dramatic irony, an audience knows something that the characters on stage do not. For example, in Shakespeare's *Othello*, Othello thinks that his wife has been sleeping with another man. All along, the audience knows that this is not true because they have seen Othello's 'friend' Iago plant false evidence.

Satire

Satire is deliberately ridiculing a person's foolishness or weaknesses, using humour, irony, or exaggeration. It's sometimes used to laugh at a corrupt society.

In 1729, Jonathan Swift published *A Modest Proposal*. His essay recommends that poor Irish people sell their children so that rich people can eat them; this way, the children won't become a burden on society. Of course, he doesn't mean it. His satirical ideas mock the heartless attitudes that some people had towards the poor. Here's an extract in which he talks about how expensive children might be to buy and eat:

Vocabulary
Dear: expensive
Devoured: eaten
Title: the right to own something (entitlement)

> *I grant this food will be somewhat dear, and therefore very proper for landlords, who, as they have already devoured most of the parents, seem to have the best title to the children.*

Parody

Parody is imitating the style of a particular writer, artist, or genre with deliberate exaggeration for comic effect. Here's an example:

> *It is a truth universally acknowledged, that a single student in possession of a good phone, must be in want of 4G coverage.*

Test Yourself!

Read each example and in the right-hand column label one of the following: verbal irony, situational irony, dramatic irony, satire and parody. Check your answers on the next page.

	Example	Answer
1.	A character on stage makes predictions about the future. The audience knows that his predictions are wrong.	
2.	It is a truth universally acknowledged, that a single ghost in possession of a body must be in want of a head.	
3.	A burglar's house is burgled.	
4.	What a beautiful day it is! (It's raining.)	
5.	The best way to deal with overpopulation is to sterilize 50% of the world.	

Fascinating Fact!

In Britain in the Middle Ages (500-1500), rhetoric was first used to spread the word of God. It was slow to get off the ground, however, as it was associated with 'heathen' Romans. Once its popularity increased, rhetoric came to be associated with religion rather than with politics.

1. Dramatic irony
2. Parody
3. Situational irony
4. Verbal irony
5. Satire (in this example, exaggeration highlights and ridicules extreme views.)

ANAPHORA

Anaphora (pronounced a-NAFF-er-uh) is the deliberate repetition of a word or phrase at the beginning of clauses. It adds rhythm and makes ideas more prominent:

> *It was the best of times, it was the worst of times, it was the age of wisdom, it was the age of foolishness, it was the epoch of belief, it was the epoch of incredulity, it was the season of Light, it was the season of Darkness, it was the spring of hope, it was the winter of despair, we had everything before us, we had nothing before us, we were all going direct to Heaven, we were all going direct the other way. . .*
>
> *—A Tale of Two Cities, Charles Dickens*

Joke Break	
Question:	What would you find in Charles Dickens's kitchen?
Answer:	The best of thymes, the worst of thymes.

Here's another example:

> *There is a time for everything, and a season for every activity under the heavens: a time to be born and a time to die, a time to plant and a time to uproot, a time to kill and a time to heal, a time to tear down and a time to build, a time to weep and a time to laugh, a time to mourn and a time to dance.*
>
> *—Bible, Ecclesiastes 3*

ANADIPLOSIS

Pronounced anna-dip-LOW-sis, anadiplosis is the repetition of a word that has just ended a sentence or clause. Anadiplosis helps the reader or listener to focus on the repeated word(s); this in turn emphasises the main idea. Here are some examples:

> *When **I give, I give** myself.*
>
> *— Song of Myself, Walt Whitman*

> *While I nodded, nearly napping, suddenly there came a tapping,*
> *As of some one gently **rapping, rapping** at my chamber door.*
>
> *— The Raven, Take Edgar Allen Poe*

This example uses anadiplosis to show how suffering can lead to hope:

> *We also rejoice in our sufferings, because we know that suffering produces **perseverance, perseverance, character;** and **character, hope.** And **hope** does not disappoint us.*
>
> *—Bible, Romans 5:3-5*

In this well-known lullaby, anadiplosis connects the lines:

> *Hush, little Baby, don't say a word,*
> *Mama's gonna buy you a **Mockingbird**.*
> *And if that **mockingbird** don't sing,*
> *Mama's gonna buy you a **diamond ring**.*
> *And if that **diamond ring** turns brass,*
> *Mama's gonna buy you a **looking glass**.*
> *And if that **looking glass** is broke,*
> *Mama's gonna buy you a **billy goat**,*
> *And if that **billy goat** won't pull,*
> *Mama's gonna buy you a **cart and a bull**.*
> *And if that **cart and bull** turn over,*
> *Mama's gonna buy you a **dog named Rover**.*
> *And if that **dog named Rover** won't bark,*
> *Mama's gonna buy you a **horse and a cart**.*
> *And if that **horse and cart** fall down,*
> *You'll still be the sweetest little baby in town.*
>
> —*Hush, Little Baby,* author and date unknown

ANTITHESIS

Antithesis is the juxtaposition or placement of contrasting ideas in **parallel clauses** (see below). It focuses the reader or listener more intensely on the contrasting ideas. For example:

> *Not that I loved Caesar less, but that I loved Rome more.*
> —*Julius Caesar,* William Shakespeare

> *To err is human; to forgive divine.*
> —*An Essay on Criticism,* Alexander Pope

> *Better to reign in Hell than serve in Heav'n.*
> —*Paradise Lost,* John Milton

ASYNDETON

Asyndeton (pronounced a-SIN-ditton) is the omission of co-ordinating conjunctions from a list. It speeds up the rhythm and engages the audience or readers, who must concentrate to work out meaning because of the missing conjunctions. For example:

> *Are all thy conquests, glories, triumphs, spoils,*
> *Shrunk to this little measure?*
> —*Julius Caesar,* William Shakespeare

> *...and that government of the people, by the people, for the people shall not perish from the Earth.*
> —Abraham Lincoln

> *These griefs, these woes, these sorrows make me old.*
> —*Romeo and Juliet,* William Shakespeare

CHIASMUS

Chiasmus is pronounced *ky* (rhyming with *sky*)-*AS-mus.* This rhetorical technique involves reversing the grammatical structure of two or more clauses for artistic effect. In chapter 14, we read these examples:

> *I wasted time, and now time doth waste me.*
> —*Richard II,* William Shakespeare

> *A fool thinks himself to be wise, but a wise man knows himself to be a fool.*
> —*As You Like It,* William Shakespeare

> *All for one, and one for all!*
> —*The Three Musketeers,* Alexandre Dumas

EPISTROPHE

Epistrophe (pronounced ep-PISS-truff-ee) is the repetition of a word or words at the **end** of successive clauses or sentences. It adds rhythm to what is said. Examples:

> *If you had known the virtue of **the ring**,*
> *Or half her worthiness that gave **the ring**,*
> *Or your own honour to contain **the ring**,*
> *You would not then have parted with **the ring**.*
> —*The Merchant of Venice,* William Shakespeare

> *Who is here so base that would be a bondman? If any, speak; **for him have I offended.** Who is here so rude that would not be a Roman? If any, speak; **for him have I offended.** Who is here so vile that will not love his country? If any, speak; **for him have I offended.***
> —*Julius Caesar,* William Shakespeare

PARALLELISM

This is the repetition of a grammatical form in a pair or series of words, phrases or clause. It creates a balanced flow of ideas. Examples:

> *It is a far, far better thing that I do, than I have ever done; it is a far, far better rest that I go to than I have ever known.*
> — *A Tale of Two Cities,* Charles Dickens

> *What the hammer? what the chain?*
> *In what furnace was thy brain?*
> *What the anvil? what dread grasp*
> *Dare its deadly terrors clasp?*
> —*The Tyger,* William Blake

> **Joke Break**
> It's a well-known fact that pencils confused Shakespeare—2B or not 2B?

POLYSYNDETON

Polysyndeton (pronounced polly-SIN-ditton) is the excessive use of co-ordinating conjunctions to join items in a list. It adds rhythm to what is being said, and the conjunctions help to focus the reader or listener on the ideas that they are connecting. For example:

> For I have neither wit, **nor** words, **nor** worth,
> Action, **nor** utterance, **nor** the power of speech,
> To stir men's blood
>
> —*Julius Caesar, William Shakespeare*

> I don't care a fig for his sense of justice—I don't care a fig for the wretchedness of London; **and** if I were young, **and** beautiful, **and** clever, **and** brilliant, **and** of a noble position, like you, I should care still less."
>
> —*The Princess Casamassima*, Henry James

> There were frowzy fields, **and** cow-houses, **and** dunghills, **and** dustheaps, **and** ditches, **and** gardens, **and** summer-houses, **and** carpet-beating grounds, at the very door of the Railway. Little tumuli of oyster shells in the oyster season, **and** of lobster shells in the lobster season, **and** of broken crockery **and** faded cabbage leaves in all seasons, encroached upon its high places.
>
> —*Dombey and Son*, Charles Dickens

TRICOLON

Tricolon (pronounced try-COAL-on) is a more sophisticated way of saying the rule of three: it refers to three words, parallel phrases or clauses that follow each other. Here are some examples:

> I explored further; **doors, doors, doors** everywhere, and all locked and bolted.
>
> —*Dracula*, Bram Stoker

The next example, the tricolon and parallelism emphasise the idea of perfect love:

> There could have been **no two hearts so open, no tastes so similar, no feelings so in unison**.
>
> —*Persuasion*, Jane Austen

Here, the tricolon, parallelism and imperative sentences emphasise the process:

> **Tell me and I forget. Teach me and I remember. Involve me and I learn.**
>
> —Benjamin Franklin

Joke Break
An Englishman, an Irishman and a teacher walk into a bar.
The teacher says, "Hold on a minute—I'm in the wrong joke!"

Test Yourself!

Read each extract in the chart on the next page. Then in the right-hand column label one of the following rhetorical devices:

Anaphora   Anadiplosis   Antithesis   Asyndeton   Chiasmus   Epistrophe
   Parallelism   Polysyndeton   Tricolon

	Example	Rhetorical Device
1.	'[I]t is respectable to have no illusions—**and** safe—**and** profitable—**and** dull.' —*Lord Jim*, Joseph Conrad	
2.	'An empty stream, a great silence, an impenetrable forest. The air was thick, warm, heavy, sluggish.' —*Heart of Darkness*, Joseph Conrad	
3.	'I love thee freely, as men strive for right. I love thee purely, as they turn from praise.' —*Sonnet 43*, Elizabeth Barrett Browning	
4.	'The world is a **comedy** to those that **think**, a **tragedy** to those that **feel**.' —Horace Walpole	
5.	'You are talking to a man who has laughed in the face of death, sneered at doom, and chuckled at catastrophe.' —*The Wizard of Oz*, L. Frank Baum	
6.	'The love of wicked men converts to **fear,** that **fear** to **hate,** and **hate** turns one or both to worthy danger and deserved death.' —*Richard II*, Shakespeare	
7.	'When I was **a child,** I spoke as **a child,** I understood as **a child,** I thought as **a child**.' —*Bible*, Corinthians 13:11	
8.	'The instinct of a man is to pursue everything that flies from him, and to fly from all that pursues him.' —*Voltaire*	
9.	'O LORD, rebuke me not in thine anger, neither chasten me in thy hot displeasure. Have mercy upon me, O LORD; for I am weak: O LORD, heal me; for my bones are vexed. My soul is also sore vexed: but thou, O LORD, how long?' —*Psalm 6*	

Check your answers on the next page.

	Example	Rhetorical Device
1.	'[I]t is respectable to have no illusions—**and** safe—**and** profitable—**and** dull.' —*Lord Jim,* Joseph Conrad	Polysyndeton (also tricolon with the adjectives)
2.	'An empty stream, a great silence, an impenetrable forest. The air was thick, warm, heavy, sluggish.' —*Heart of Darkness,* Joseph Conrad	asyndeton
3.	'I love thee freely, as men strive for right. I love thee purely, as they turn from praise.' —*Sonnet 43,* Elizabeth Barrett Browning	Parallelism (also anaphora with 'I love thee')
4.	'The world is a **comedy** to those that **think**, a **tragedy** to those that **feel**.' —Horace Walpole	antithesis (also parallelism)
5.	'You are talking to a man who has laughed in the face of death, sneered at doom, and chuckled at catastrophe.' —*The Wizard of Oz,* L. Frank Baum	tricolon (also parallelism)
6.	'The love of wicked men converts to **fear,** that **fear** to **hate**, and **hate** turns one or both to worthy danger and deserved death.' —*Richard II,* Shakespeare	anadiplosis
7.	'When I was **a child,** I spoke as **a child,** I understood as **a child,** I thought as **a child**.' —*Bible,* Corinthians 13:11	epistrophe
8.	'The instinct of a man is to pursue everything that flies from him, and to fly from all that pursues him.' —*Voltaire*	chiasmus
9.	'O LORD, rebuke me not in thine anger, neither chasten me in thy hot displeasure. Have mercy upon me, O LORD; for I am weak: O LORD, heal me; for my bones are vexed. My soul is also sore vexed: but thou, O LORD, how long?' —*Psalm 6*	anaphora

TO CONCLUDE

Well done for reaching the end of this guide to grammar, punctuation and spelling! If you completed the bonus chapter, this is particularly impressive. Just a reminder to be selective when you experiment with these rhetorical devices—as I stated earlier in the chapter, if you try to memorise and use all of them, you risk producing a contrived piece of writing that is over-stylised and lacks fluency.

Be convincing: less is more!

Outside the classroom, the ability to craft your ideas will always be an important life skill. Rhetorical devices will help you in discussions and debates, particularly when you are trying to win others around to your point of view.

Let's finish with a final *Fascinating Fact!*

Fascinating Fact!
Read this sentence: She told him that she loved him. Now add the word *only* to as many places as possible. Read your sentences out loud, changing the intonation as necessary. How many subtly different meanings can you create?

The aim of the final *Fascinating Fact!* is to encourage you to play with language.

Never stop playing: language is for life—not just for English exams!

***

If you've enjoyed this book, please feel free to review it on www.Amazon.co.uk or to follow its author Kerry Lewis on Twitter @Mrs_SPaG.

Printed in Great Britain
by Amazon